THE PARTNERING INTELLIGENCE FIELDBOOK

Create Magical Partnerships!

Mike

The
PARTNERING
intelligence
Fieldbook

Tools and Techniques for

Building Strong Alliances

for Your Business

STEPHEN M. DENT *and* SANDRA M. NAIMAN

DAVIES-BLACK PUBLISHING
Palo Alto, California

Published by Davies-Black Publishing, a division of CPP, Inc., 3803 East Bayshore Road, Palo Alto, CA 94303; 800-624-1765.

Special discounts on bulk quantities of Davies-Black books are available to corporations, professional associations, and other organizations. For details, contact the Director of Book Marketing and Sales at Davies-Black Publishing, 3803 East Bayshore Road, Palo Alto, CA 94303; 650-691-9123; fax 650-623-9271.

Visit the Davies-Black Publishing web site at www.davies-black.com.

06 05 04 03 02   10 9 8 7 6 5 4 3 2 1
Printed in the United States of America

Library of Congress Cataloging-in-Publication Data
Dent, Stephen M.
  The partnering intelligence fieldbook : tools and techniques for building strong alliances for your business / Stephen M. Dent and Sandra M. Naiman.—1st ed.
     p. cm.
  Includes index.
  ISBN 0-89106-166-5 (pbk.)
  1. Strategic alliances (Business) 2. Business networks. I. Naiman, Sandra M. II. Title.

HD69.S8 D465 2002
658´.044—dc21

2002023415

FIRST EDITION
First printing 2002

To the many clients I have worked with
since the release of Partnering Intelligence.
The lessons I have learned from them have been enormous,
and I can only hope I have given back half as much in return.
Stephen M. Dent

To my children, Cory and Whitney.
They have become admirable and caring adults
who bless me with their constant presence in my life,
keeping me forever young and smiling.
Sandra M. Naiman

CONTENTS

ACKNOWLEDGMENTS

I want to thank Sandra Naiman for her contributions to the fieldbook. I would also like to acknowledge and express my grateful appreciation to Laurie Harper, our agent, who worked hard to make this book possible, as well as to Al Diaz of NASA, Mary Lou Cagle of Bank of America, Mike Salvino of Exult, Tom Raffio of NE Delta Dental, Susan Schaefer of Qwest International, Judy Kessel of StoneArch Creative, and the many others who provided insights. I especially want to thank my colleagues Phyl Burger, Thomas Quill, Cindy Browne, Dean DeGroot, and Nancy Cosgriff, and our transatlantic partners at ServQ Ltd., Andrew Crossley and Ian Watson. Finally, thanks to Neal Holtan, M.D., for his unconditional love and support in all my efforts.

Stephen M. Dent

First, I want to thank Stephen Dent for the invitation to contribute to the fieldbook. I am grateful to my colleagues Rich Blakeman, Jim Krefft, and Tim Schroeder for their unlimited patience and invaluable contributions of time and insights. Laurie Harper, our agent, went far beyond the call of duty to bring this book to market, and I so appreciate the generous contribution of her valuable time. Connie Kallback, Jill Anderson-Wilson, and others at Davies-Black were ready and willing to do whatever was necessary during the publishing process. I thank them all for their responsiveness, professionalism, and hard work. Finally, I thank Sylvia Baumgarten and Helen Pringle for their unconditional support and for always believing in me.

Sandra M. Naiman

Every person or team using this fieldbook has the potential to be a great partner. We are naturally wired to want to work together. This is how we as a species have survived throughout our history. Enormous hardships such as climatic change, famine, wars, and plagues have not prevented us from prospering; arguably, the world is a safer, healthier, and wealthier place today than ever before.

One of the most important factors in moving humankind forward has been our ability to partner. While we can all cite examples of failed partnerships, thousands of successful partnering endeavors have improved lives and living conditions for all of us. Individual genius may exist in a Mozart or an Einstein, but most of humankind's achievements have been the result of people working together—a proven strategy for success.

Yet, being a great partner is not easy. In fact it often requires us to act in ways counter to what we have been taught and how we are socialized. We spend our formative years being dependent on our caregivers. Craving independence, we bound from the confines of our homes and families as soon as we are able—to be on our own and free to make our own choices. Our independence is rewarded as we are recognized for who we are and what we accomplish in school, clubs, sports, the arts, and other personal endeavors.

Partnering requires us to put aside our desires for immediate and instant self-gratification. Smart partners know that to be a great partner, you must understand and work hard to satisfy your partner's needs, and that in the process you will also get your needs met. It takes a huge leap of faith to believe that if you work hard to satisfy your partner's needs, he or she will work hard to satisfy yours. For this to happen, all the partners involved must have high Partnering Intelligence—the ability to create a partnering culture.

In this fieldbook, we offer you a step-by-step guide in how to use the Partnership Continuum™ model. The model comprises two separate yet intertwined and concurrent processes known as the Stages of Relationship Development and the Stages of Partnership Development. The Stages of

Relationship Development—Form, Storm, Norm, and Perform—describe the behavioral cycle people travel to establish trust with each other in order to work well together. The Stages of Partnership Development—Assess, Explore, Initiate, and Commit—describe the steps required to build the partnership.

To benefit from these two sets of development stages, and to create a successful partnering culture, each partner, or potential partner, must be adept in the use of the behavioral skills known as the Six Partnering Attributes™, which include:

- Self-Disclosure and Feedback

- Win-Win Orientation

- Ability to Trust

- Future Orientation

- Comfort with Change

- Comfort with Interdependence

These skills are designed to provide you with personal insights and competencies you'll need to be able to navigate through the Stages of Relationship Development. Mastery of the Six Partnering Attributes is the goal of smart partners and smart organizations, creating an environment that allows trust to take root and flourish. This is critical if partners are to believe that each person is working hard to get the other's needs met.

Part One of this fieldbook is designed to help individuals understand and increase their competencies and skills in the Stages of Relationship Development, which are embodied in the Six Partnering Attributes. In Part Two we review the Partnership Continuum model and focus on the Stages of Partnership Development. This portion of the book is designed to be worked on in small groups.

Improving one's own Partnering Intelligence and following a deliberate and purposeful partnering process are the two crucial elements of building smart partnerships.

Stephen M. Dent is an internationally renowned author and consultant, and founding principal of Minneapolis-based Partnership Continuum, Inc. Through his research and application of the Partnership Continuum model, he has helped organizations such as NASA, Bank of America, Exult, Xcel Energy, Girl Scouts of the USA, and hundreds of others form award-winning, sustainable, and profitable alliances and partnerships. This fieldbook is based on his book *Partnering Intelligence: Creating Value for Your Business by Building Strong Alliances*. You can learn more about Dent and his work at www.partneringintelligence.com.

Sandra M. Naiman is a principal of Topline Associates, Inc., a Denver-based consulting firm specializing in helping clients accelerate revenue growth through business planning; selection, retention, and development of top talent; and achieving sales results through sales process improvement, activity management, and partnering. She has worked throughout the United States, Canada, Mexico, and Europe with clients such as Sun Microsystems, J. P. Morgan, Kellogg Corporation, Lockheed Martin, Ford, and Exxon Mobil.

PART ONE

ASSESSING YOUR
ABILITY TO PARTNER

"The better I get, the better we get" sums up our approach to creating great partnerships. While many of us bemoan the problems we have with partners, we rarely look to ourselves as contributors to those problems. Yet, the only part of the relationship we can truly control is ourself. Learning how to be a smart partner is the first step in building great partnerships.

Part One explains how to become a smart partner. You'll want to do this for two reasons. First, you'll be a better partner in the long run, not just in your professional life. Partnering skills are life skills: they work for you in your personal, family, and community lives. Second, all groups go through the Stages of Relationship Development. These predictable stages—Form, Storm, Norm, and Perform—are the steps in a cycle people use to determine trust and move from skepticism to performance. The Six Partnering Attributes help you and your partners move through this cycle more efficiently and successfully.

We begin in Chapter 1 by providing you with the Partnering Quotient (PQ) Assessment to measure your Partnering Intelligence. This validated instrument has been used by thousands of people just like you. It provides you with a "raw PQ score" and then breaks the score down based on the Six Partnering Attributes.

The Six Partnering Attributes are the critical skills that build an environment of trust. Partnerships are organic in nature and thus are nurtured or threatened by the atmosphere in which they live. Each of the Six Partnering Attributes is an element in that atmosphere.

Understanding and becoming adept in the use of the Six Partnering Attributes forms the first step in becoming a smart partner. Once you've completed the PQ Assessment, you are ready to tackle each of the attributes separately. Based on what you've learned, perhaps you'll want to start with the areas in which you are weakest, then move to those areas in which you have strength to reinforce what you are currently doing to build your relationships. Or, you may just want to start with the first attribute and work your way through all six.

However you choose to use the fieldbook, Part One is packed with assessments, tools, and tips that are sure to help you improve your ability to partner—your Partnering Intelligence. It is designed for individual use, but many of the tools work equally well in a team or group setting. If it's appropriate, try using the tools as a team. Pick a tool or assessment of interest and work through it together. It's a great way to gain insights into how others in the partnership think, feel, and behave.

There is no right or wrong way to use this fieldbook. The important thing is to pick it up and use it. It's an indispensable tool for bringing you and your organization the value and benefits of great partnerships.

What Does It Take to Be a Smart Partner?

A partnership is where two or more people work together to accomplish a goal or task while building trust and a mutually beneficial relationship. In a successful partnership, a clearly defined and tangible outcome of the partnership is agreed upon; the process of accomplishing this outcome builds trust between the partners; and all partners are clear about the value they gain from—and bring to—the relationship.

Examples of Partnerships

Two People in a Business Setting

John is vice president of engineering in a national wireless telephone company. His responsibilities include making sure that service is available to customers and managing the site construction budget. He must deal with the many requests to build sites, mostly in suburban areas that have "blind spots"—areas where wireless phones drop calls, frustrating customers.

Sue is vice president of marketing and sales. She is responsible for identifying customers' needs and providing solutions that keep customers loyal to the company's products. She is also responsible for building the customer subscriber base and increasing the retention of new customers.

Sue's customer research indicates that customers want a "backbone" of service provided along interstate highways so that as they travel between cities, they can talk on their phones. She asks John to partner with her to develop a plan to build wireless "cell sites" along one of the major interstate highways that connects two of their most important markets. While John prefers to fill blind spots within certain suburban areas of their major markets, he agrees to work with Sue to meet both their needs. Together they build a mutually agreeable cell site deployment plan that balances the building of sites within suburban areas with accelerating interstate site construction. This win-win approach allows them to meet their objectives while attracting and keeping customers who travel between their respective markets.

Two Businesses Working Together

A major international airline wants to offer regional cuisine from the airline's hub cities to its customers. Research indicates that customers prefer these specialized foods over foods from "national" brands, which tend to be predictable and less "exotic."

A local bakery in one of the airline's headquarter cities would like to extend its market brand and increase production beyond the metropolitan areas it serves. The bakery does not have the economic capacity to build a production and distribution network to accomplish this objective. It does, however, make the best banana-nut and blueberry muffins in the world.

Mike, the head of in-flight catering for the airline, loves those muffins. He contacts the owner of the bakery, Jeanette, to inquire how the airline might start offering Jeanette's muffins on morning breakfast flights. Jeanette tells Mike that she would love the business but she lacks the resources to bake and package the number required by the airline.

Mike and Jeanette come up with an idea. If the airline would provide Jeanette with a low-interest loan to increase capacity, and a two-year contract for muffins, would Jeanette be willing to invest in upgrading her business? The answer is yes, and within six months the airline is serving the best morning muffins in the sky and saving money in the process. Meanwhile, Jeanette is getting inquiries about her muffins from people who are eating them with their morning coffee on flights all over the world.

A Team Working on a Project

An international automobile manufacturer is in the process of developing a "world car," one that could be manufactured and sold on several different continents. The company staff puts together a design team that consists of members from Asia, South America, North America, and Europe. The team agrees to meet in Toronto to discuss how they will work together to build this new car. Each member is asked to bring regional consumer requirements for input.

At their meeting, the design team agrees that to be successful, the members must partner with each other and build trust. Some members express fears that their production facilities might not be reengineered to build the new cars. Their fears turn out to be well founded. Some car manufacturers aren't interested in building redundant production facilities. Therefore, how the car is to be designed becomes an important factor in deciding which regions get to build the cars.

After intensive review of consumer needs, preliminary design sketches are presented that contain a variety of consistent components. A final design is selected. At this point, the team needs to recommend where the car should be manufactured. Several locations in various countries including England, Germany, United States, Canada, Mexico, Brazil, China, and Thailand are competing with one another.

The team agrees to do an analysis of strengths and weaknesses of each location. With the objective being to make the endeavor beneficial for all members of the team, and to build the car as cost-effectively as possible, the team resolves the problem using a unique formula. The cars are to be assembled in England, Canada, Brazil, and Thailand, and the other sites are to manufacture important components for the automobile such as transmissions, chassis, and engines. Each region receives a share of the work according to its specific area of excellence. The amount of plant reengineering is minimal, which saves millions for the company, and each continent has an assembly plant, minimizing transportation costs.

Two Individuals

Two friends, Peter and Jason, decide to go mountain climbing together. Peter wants to go to the Rocky Mountains in Colorado, while Jason has his heart set on the Dolomites in northern Italy. "There's no culture in Colorado," complains Jason; to him, the chance to stop off in Venice is a real plus. But Peter has no interest in going all the way to Italy to climb mountains. The disagreement seems insurmountable.

Being good partners, they sit down and look at each others' secondary needs. Peter needs to stay within a budget. He feels they could keep expenses to a minimum by camping in Colorado. Jason wants an exotic, foreign experience.

They do some research and discover that when they consider all the costs—airline flights, food, and accommodations—they can climb in Peru for less than in Colorado and for less than half of what Italy would cost. Peter gets a big bargain, and Jason gets an exotic vacation climbing in the Andes.

When they get home, they both agree they had the vacation of a lifetime. The friends are now planning their next climb.

Action Step In the exercise below, identify the tangible outcome of the partnership, the value that each partner contributed, and how each partner benefited from the relationship for each of the four examples just described. Then, think about these partnerships in relation to your own experience.

LEARNING FROM EXAMPLE

Example 1: Two People in a Business Setting

Outcome: _____

Value contributed by each partner: _____

Benefit to each partner: _____

Example 2: Two Businesses Working Together

Outcome: _____

Value contributed by each partner: _____

Benefit to each partner: _____

Example 3: A Team Working on a Project

Outcome: _____

Value contributed by each partner: _____

Benefit to each partner: _____

Example 4: Two Individuals

Outcome: _____

Value contributed by each partner: _____

Benefit to each partner: _____

Partnering As an Activity

The true measure of a partnership lies not only in what is accomplished, but also in the way things get done. Partners relate to each other in a way that reflects mutual respect, trust, and accountability.

Partnerships Are Entered Into Voluntarily

Partnerships cannot be forced. However, we often find ourselves in situations where we are "assigned" to partners—for example, when we are appointed to a project or task force, join an existing board of directors, work on a committee at a school, or volunteer to help plan the church picnic. In these cases, relationships can become true partnerships only when all involved have defined the goal or task, have identified the mutual benefits, and are committed to building trust.

Partners Perceive Themselves to Be Equal in Power and Accountability

In a partnership, authority and title are meaningless in the delegation of tasks, decision making, and conflict resolution. The only factors that might make one partner's perspective take precedence over another's are greater knowledge or more experience. How roles and responsibilities are assigned depends on the demands of the situation and the particular competencies of the partners.

For example, let's say the sales organization of a large telecommunications company needs a training strategy for new hires and tenured employees. A consulting partner is hired to provide the strategy to be implemented internally by the client organization. In determining the selection of project manager, the consulting organization selects a person with a strong sales background. Close support to the manager is provided by a partner with an extensive training and development background. Later on, when the focus changes to ongoing professional development, their roles may shift.

Partners Have Equal Access to, and Openly Share, Information and Knowledge

In a partnership the emphasis is always on the task or outcome for which the partners came together in the first place. To that end, all partners need to have access to the same information. In corporate settings, individuals often operate according to the adage that "knowledge is power," and they increase their power by hoarding information, parceling out bits and pieces as needed. In a partnership, however, partners are not focused on power. All partners are perceived as equal and therefore willingly share information. This not only enhances the functioning of the partnership, it also increases the quality of the outcome. Synergy and creativity result when people build upon one another's information and ideas.

All Partners Are Perceived As Equally Valuable, Albeit in Different Ways

Partnerships come together when individuals require the contribution of others to accomplish a task or reach a goal. By definition, every partner has something of value to bring to the partnership, and that something is essential to the quality of the outcome. Therefore, every partner is acknowledged for the value of his or her contribution, and no one partner is viewed as more important than any other.

Partners Look for Opportunities to Discover They Are Wrong

When all partners are committed to the excellence of the outcome, they want to continually check that their perceptions, decisions, and actions will produce the best product or service. To that end, they welcome suggestions about how to do things differently. Indeed, they actively seek them out! Partners don't want to be "right" or have the last word. They want to arrive at the best possible outcome or solution and are open to any and all information that will help them achieve it.

Partners Seek Out and Support Success for Others

Partners bring to a relationship an outlook of *abundance.* An individual with an abundant outlook believes that there is enough of everything available in the world for everyone to get what he or she needs. There is enough money. There is enough success. There is enough recognition. There is enough love and affection. People who possess an abundant outlook can seek opportunities for others to succeed and can celebrate others' successes because they know this does not detract from their opportunities to be successful as well.

People whose outlook is one of *scarcity* feel that anything that goes to anyone else takes something from them. They therefore are unable to promote or support the success of others because they covet it for themselves. Such individuals have great difficulty working in partnerships.

Think about a partnership in which you are currently engaged and answer the questions in the exercise below. What conclusions can you draw about this partnership?

PARTNERSHIP DYNAMICS	
1. What is the purpose of the partnership?	
2. What are the benefits from this relationship for each partner?	
3. What is working well in the partnership? What could work better?	
4. What contributions do you make to the partnership? What contributions does your partner make?	
5. How are decisions made?	
6. How are disagreements settled?	
7. What information is shared? How is it shared?	
8. How do you and your partner contribute to one another's success?	
9. On a scale of 1 to 10, with 10 being the highest, how would you rate the success of the partnership?	

Measuring Your Partnering Intelligence: The PQ Assessment

The Partnering Quotient (PQ) Assessment is a tool that increases your awareness of your Partnering Intelligence. This inventory identifies potential strengths and weaknesses and reflects how you perceive yourself based on the attributes of Partnering Intelligence.

Partnering Intelligence is a situational intelligence. The more trust you feel in a relationship, the higher your Partnering Intelligence will be. In situations where there is little or no trust, you will have a lower PQ. In emotional situations, we typically revert to past behaviors that have proven successful. However, these past solutions may have met some short-term need that no longer exists. Smart partners want to understand the current situation and respond using new and successful strategies. The PQ Assessment will help you identify past ways of resolving problems and provide options for new solutions.

> **Action Step**   **To gain a better understanding of your partnering skills, complete the PQ Assessment on the following pages.**

THE PQ ASSESSMENT

- **The PQ Assessment is not a test with right or wrong answers.** The PQ Assessment provides an accurate portrayal of your strengths and weaknesses in a partnering situation. It is designed to help you enhance your ability to be a smart partner. Consider it a snapshot of yourself at a particular point in time. You can look at a photograph of yourself and think: "I look pretty good; I like what I see." Or you can think: "Gee, I didn't realize I could stand up straighter. In the future, I want to pull my shoulders back more." Similarly, you can look at the results of your PQ Assessment and decide you want to enhance some aspect of your behavior in partnerships.

- **The PQ Assessment is descriptive, not evaluative.** We are all products of our history and learn from experience. Our behavior reflects beliefs, attitudes, and orientations that have worked for us before. The PQ Assessment describes your beliefs, attitudes, and orientation toward partnering. The instrument itself is not meant to evaluate them. Rather, it provides you with a profile that you can use in current or future relationships to enhance the effectiveness of a partnership.

Directions

- Use the following scale to score each statement:

    1 = Strongly Agree
    2 = Agree
    3 = Somewhat Agree
    4 = Somewhat Disagree
    5 = Disagree
    6 = Strongly Disagree

- Enter your score in the column to the right of each statement *and* in the shaded box on the same line.

- When responding, pick a context from either your work life or home life. Think about how you typically react in the situation described in the statement. Do not contemplate a statement for too long. Your initial response is likely to be the most accurate.

- Score the statements as honestly as you can. The extent to which this tool is useful depends upon how accurately it reflects what is actually true for you.

THE PQ ASSESSMENT (CONTINUED)

1 = Strongly Agree 2 = Agree 3 = Somewhat Agree 4 = Somewhat Disagree 5 = Disagree 6 = Strongly Disagree

Statement	Score	A	B	C	D	E	F
1. I believe a person's behavior stays the same over time.					▓		
2. I like to do familiar tasks.						▓	
3. People tell me I'm inclined to be a competitive person.			▓				
4. When I'm with other people, I always make sure my needs are met first.							▓
5. In general, I like it when everyone follows the rules.						▓	
6. I like to depend on myself to get things done.							▓
7. People need to prove I can trust them.				▓			
8. I feel uncomfortable sharing my feelings with others.		▓					
9. I believe that actions speak louder than words.				▓			
10. I get frustrated being on a team.							▓
11. I tend to make decisions about someone based on what he or she has done before.					▓		
12. I feel very anxious when I'm in a new situation.						▓	
13. If I don't win a conflict, I feel upset.			▓				
14. When I need to go somewhere, I prefer to depend on myself to get there.							▓
15. I like to have people prove their facts.				▓			
Subtotal							

1 = Strongly Agree   2 = Agree   3 = Somewhat Agree   4 = Somewhat Disagree   5 = Disagree   6 = Strongly Disagree

Statement	Score	A	B	C	D	E	F
16. I believe in keeping my personal life to myself.		▓					
17. Past history is a better predictor of events than a future plan.					▓		
18. I get very nervous when I meet new people.						▓	
19. I prefer to use techniques I've used before to accomplish new tasks.			▓				
20. I'd rather give in to another's wishes than argue for my point.			▓				
21. I rarely share family information with others.		▓					
22. I think it's important to check up on people to make sure they do what they say they'll do.				▓			
23. I will give up something important to me to reach a compromise.			▓				
24. I get upset when people tell me something about myself that I don't like.		▓					
25. I am more interested in actualities than I am in possibilities.					▓		
26. I prefer a signed contract to a handshake agreement.				▓			
27. I like having my day planned and scheduled and get frustrated when I have to change it.							
28. I feel I am more private than outgoing.		▓					
29. I would rather be by myself than spend time with other people.							▓
30. In an argument, being right is more important than maintaining the other person's dignity.			▓				
Subtotal							
Page 12 Subtotal							
Total Score							

The PQ Assessment Score Sheet

Your Partnering Quotient (PQ) measures how you perceive yourself in the six attributes that form Partnering Intelligence. Your score can be used to identify potential strengths and weaknesses, but the primary purpose of the survey is to increase your self-awareness.

Your Partnering Quotient

To obtain your PQ, subtotal the scores in the *first* column ("Score") on each page of the assessment, combine the subtotals, and enter the total score here.

   Total Score _____

Rankings

   131–180: High PQ
   81–130: Medium PQ
   30–80:   Low PQ

The Six Attributes of Partnering Intelligence

To obtain your average score for each of the six attributes, subtotal the scores in the shaded boxes in *each* column (A–F), enter the total scores at the bottom of page 13 and to the right of each attribute column here, and then divide by 5.

	Total	Average
Column A: Self-Disclosure and Feedback	_____ /5 =	_____
Column B: Win-Win Orientation	_____ /5 =	_____
Column C: Ability to Trust	_____ /5 =	_____
Column D: Future Orientation	_____ /5 =	_____
Column E: Comfort with Change	_____ /5 =	_____
Column F: Comfort with Interdependence	_____ /5 =	_____

Referring to the sample on the next page, transfer your average scores to the Attribute Analysis Grid that follows.

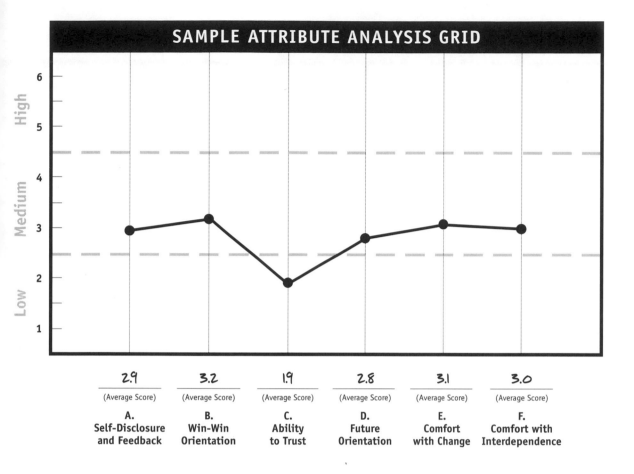

SAMPLE ATTRIBUTE ANALYSIS GRID

2.9	3.2	1.9	2.8	3.1	3.0
(Average Score)	(Average Score)	(Average Score)	(Average Score)	(Average Score)	(Average Score)
A. Self-Disclosure and Feedback	**B.** Win-Win Orientation	**C.** Ability to Trust	**D.** Future Orientation	**E.** Comfort with Change	**F.** Comfort with Interdependence

The Attribute Analysis Grid gives a personal PQ profile of your current level of competency in all six attributes. It visually displays how you scored in each of the separate attributes and can help you focus on areas you want to improve.

To Complete the Grid

Start with the first attribute, Self-Disclosure and Feedback. Note your average score by putting a dot in the appropriate place on the first vertical line. Continue until you have plotted all six attributes. Once that's completed, connect the dots to get a profile of your overall ranking. Note that the vertical lines are divided into three sections: low, medium, and high. Each reflects how often you demonstrate the attribute, based on how you responded to the statements in the PQ Assessment.

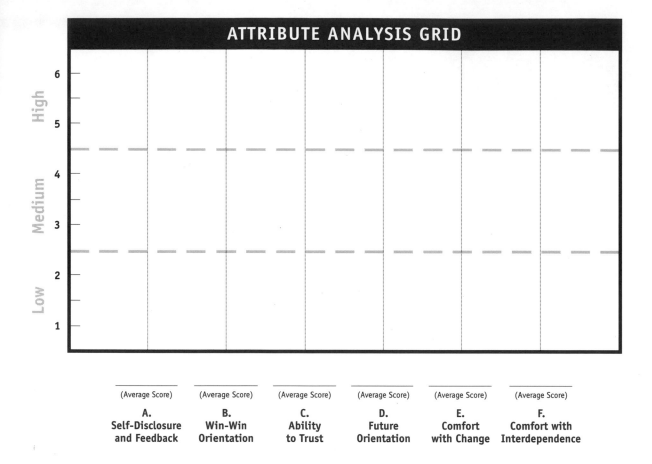

ATTRIBUTE ANALYSIS GRID

	(Average Score)	(Average Score)	(Average Score)	(Average Score)	(Average Score)	(Average Score)
	A. Self-Disclosure and Feedback	**B.** Win-Win Orientation	**C.** Ability to Trust	**D.** Future Orientation	**E.** Comfort with Change	**F.** Comfort with Interdependence

To Interpret the Grid

First note the areas in which you scored high, or high relative to the others. These represent your current strengths in partnering. Next, examine those areas that are low, or lower than the others. These are areas that you might want to improve. Each of the six attributes is an important factor in the efficiency of the system as a whole.

The Six Partnering Attributes of Partnering Intelligence

No matter the score, we can all strive to improve our ability to partner. Simply taking the PQ Assessment enhances your awareness of your behaviors as they relate to the Six Partnering Attributes of Partnering Intelligence.

Self-Disclosure and Feedback looks at your comfort level in providing others with information about yourself. It also indicates how comfortable you feel about giving feedback about others. In order to get your needs met, you must be willing to share them with others, and others need to know how you think and feel about what they disclose to you. Trust grows and everyone benefits from the relationship when Self-Disclosure and Feedback occurs in a partnership. If you scored high on this attribute, you are also likely to have scored high on Comfort with Interdependence and Win-Win Orientation.

If you scored low on Self-Disclosure and Feedback, the extent to which you benefit from, and contribute to, a partnership will be more limited over time. If you are not getting what you need from a relationship, resentment and anger build, and you may have a tendency to sabotage the ultimate effectiveness of the partnership.

Win-Win Orientation measures the extent to which you seek a win-win outcome to problem solving and conflict resolution. If you have a high Win-Win Orientation, you like to ensure that each party in a partnership gets his or her needs met. You are probably assertive without being overbearing, and while you don't seek conflict, you most likely are not afraid of it.

If you scored low on this attribute, you probably use a win-lose problem-solving and conflict resolution style. This is the case with people who tend to avoid conflict or with those who are competitive. People who define conflict as "bad" or threatening will give in to the needs of others rather than speak up for their own needs. Individuals who are competitive often believe that for them to win, someone else has to lose. In a partnership, effectiveness is severely undermined if one or more of the partners feel that they are in a losing situation.

Ability to Trust is your confidence that others will do as they promise and will behave in a straightforward manner. If you scored high on this attribute, you operate on the premise that "what you see is what you get." This is true for yourself, and you assume the same for others. You probably give trust automatically and spend very little time worrying about whether others will deliver as promised. You see no need to "watch your back."

If you scored low on Ability to Trust, you probably believe that trust must be earned. Therefore, in the absence of a long history during which this can occur, you might be skeptical of others, withhold information, and prefer to do everything yourself.

Future Orientation refers to the extent to which you focus on a vision of the future and set your expectations with that vision in mind. If you scored high on Future Orientation, you probably use a planning style and then hold yourself and others accountable for keeping commitments. You do not rely on past history to make decisions about future expectations.

If you scored low on this attribute, it will be difficult for you to believe that circumstances in your future can be any different from what they were in your past. If you have been disappointed in past or current partners, you might expect to be disappointed in them again. This assumption stifles any hope that things can be different and greatly reduces the possibility that they will be.

Comfort with Change refers to the extent to which you like, adapt to, and even embrace change. If you scored high on this attribute, you seek out opportunities to do different things and to do things differently. You are open to the ideas of others and are alert to new and better ways of approaching people, situations, and tasks.

If you scored low on this attribute, you probably like to do things the way they have been done in the past. You may be uncomfortable trying new things or new ways of doing familiar things. People who are uncomfortable with change tend to stick to the status quo.

Comfort with Interdependence refers to the extent to which you can rely on others for your success. In partnerships, people plan together and then perform according to plan. Tasks are divided between the partners, and then each is accountable for delivering on his or her commitments. If you scored high on Comfort with Interdependence, you focus on doing your best work and allow your partner to do the same.

If you scored low on this attribute, you are probably a great individual contributor. You are likely to function best when you have complete control over a situation and perform all the required tasks yourself. In a partnership situation, you may go off on a tangent, leaving others lost or bewildered. If you are not comfortable being interdependent, you may find partnering difficult.

Understanding the PQ Assessment Statements

Each statement on the PQ Assessment reflects an attribute. No one attribute stands alone, nor does a statement necessarily reflect only one attribute. For instance, if you have a low Ability to Trust, you may have difficulty creating a Win-Win Orientation because you may believe your partners will not uphold their agreement. To increase your Partnering Intelligence, you need to reflect on your ability to master all six attributes.

If you wish to better understand your score on any or all of the attributes, review the following statements and the attributes they reflect. Use a highlighter to note any parts of the interpretation that particularly apply to you.

Self-Disclosure and Feedback

8. I feel uncomfortable sharing my feelings with others.

The ability to disclose information about oneself creates an important dynamic for successful partnerships. Self-disclosure creates a sense of openness between the parties. This enables each party to communicate important information about their needs and provides opportunities to give feedback. This important communication skill is a trust-building device that creates a powerful bond moving the partnership toward achieving its objectives.

16. I believe in keeping my personal life to myself.

We are the same at work as we are at home. We may alter the façade, but our core being and values do not change. When we hide a part of ourselves from others, people sense we are not being fully genuine. This starts a cycle of mistrust: if you don't share fully with me, then I am reluctant to share fully with you.

21. I rarely share family information with others.

While we all have boundaries between our personal and business lives, it is normal to talk about our spouse, significant other, children, and outside activities and hobbies. People who are so closed that they cannot share family information send a message to others that is generally perceived as mistrust and a lack of candor. People respond to this message by shutting down communication themselves. This ultimately will hurt the partnership.

24. I get upset when people tell me something about myself that I don't like.

When we hear comments or feedback we don't like, frequently it means the feedback has hit a nerve. We may inwardly acknowledge a trait yet outwardly deny it. The ability to accept feedback is closely associated with self-disclosure. Remembering that feedback reflects as much on the giver as it does on the receiver may make it easier to be open to feedback from others.

28. I feel I am more private than outgoing.

If you are a private person, you may be sending signals to partners that you are uncomfortable disclosing information about yourself or your needs. While it simply may be that you are introverted, your ability to provide information to your partners is crucial if trust is to be established. Early on you may want to address your personality style with partners to ensure there are no misunderstandings. If you want trust to grow, be clear and upfront about your needs and provide feedback to your partners.

Action Step   **Upon review of the statements that reflect your level of Self-Disclosure and Feedback:**

• What did you learn about yourself in regard to this attribute?

_____

_____

• How do you think your level of Self-Disclosure and Feedback influences your behavior in partnerships?

_____

_____

Win-Win Orientation

3. People tell me I'm inclined to be a competitive person.

Competitively driven people focus on creating situations where they can win. While sometimes this helps them succeed, it can be a liability in a partnership, where the focus needs to switch from a competitive win-lose dynamic to a collaborative win-win approach. To get everyone's needs met, all parties must work together. Competitive behavior is an indicator of low Comfort with Interdependence. The nature of competition means "you go it alone" to win.

13. If I don't win a conflict, I feel upset.

Competitive people need to win conflicts; if they do not, they feel bad. But your Partnering Intelligence increases when you are able to create a win-win resolution within your partnership. Also, if you define changing as "losing," you will feel resentment when a partnership requires you to do something differently. This statement may also reflect a past orientation. When competitive people win a conflict, they feel they can control the situation and need not build on a mutually agreeable plan for the future.

20. I'd rather give in to another's wishes than argue for my point.

When a person is always accommodating another's wishes, resentment inevitability builds. When this resentment reaches a critical stage, the person begins to act it out, often resulting in sabotage. He or she will act as though there is agreement and collaboration but will undermine all attempts to accomplish the task or objective of the partnership.

23. I will give up something important to me to reach a compromise.

Contrary to what many believe, a compromise by definition sets up either a lose-lose or a lose-win dynamic. In either case, if you give up something important to you, ultimately it will come back to haunt you. Usually in a compromise situation, both parties lose the energy to resolve a conflict in a collaborative way. Rather than give in to compromise, it's most effective to create a new solution in which both parties win.

30. In an argument, being right is more important than maintaining the other person's dignity.

If it is so important that you be right in an argument that you would sacrifice another person's dignity to do so, it is unlikely that you are using a win-win style of conflict resolution. It is important when resolving conflicts to be sure your partners feel they have also won. Being right is less important than affording other human beings the respect and dignity they deserve.

**Action Step** **Upon review of the statements that reflect your Win-Win Orientation:**

• What did you learn about yourself in regard to this attribute?

_____

_____

• How do you think your Win-Win Orientation influences your behavior in partnerships?

_____

_____

Ability to Trust

7. People need to prove I can trust them.

Some people trust freely, others need to build trust, and some people never learn to trust at all. If you need people to constantly "prove" themselves to you, then you probably have a low Ability to Trust. This may also mean you make decisions about people based on what they have demonstrated to you in the past. If they have disappointed you, you will continue to have low expectations and trust.

9. I believe that actions speak louder than words.

People who consistently do what they say they are going to do build trust. If a person says one thing and does something else, he or she may not have felt enough trust in a partnership to openly disclose their real intentions. If you cannot take a person at his or her word, then most probably you are basing that decision on an event in the past in which you were disappointed. This may indicate a decision-making style based on past history.

15. I like to have people prove their facts.

While knowing the facts is not a bad thing, if you are able to believe someone without seeing the facts for yourself, this demonstrates your Ability to Trust. In relationships, a person's feelings and perceptions are also facts, in that they represent information important to the outcome of the partnership. Many business partnerships move to quantum improvements when decisions are based on intuitive knowledge and feelings. How are you going to prove the facts in those situations? This statement may also indicate discomfort with change. When you want to see the facts, you may not be willing to change without extensive reasons for doing so.

22. I think it is important to check up on people to make sure they do what they say they'll do.

When you do not trust that people will do what they say they'll do, you feel compelled to check up on them. This statement might also reveal a past orientation. If someone has disappointed you in the past, you may try to make sure that individual lives up to future agreements.

26. I prefer a signed contract to a handshake agreement.

If you have negotiated your partnership with openness and honesty, by the time negotiations are completed a handshake should seal the agreement. If you still need the security of a signed legal document, then perhaps you do not trust your partner. You might want to check out your Ability to Trust. Although it is often prudent to have documented and legally binding agreements, such agreements can occur after a partnership is formed. If you have lawyers in when you are first exploring a partnership, you might want to think about whether you truly trust your prospective partner.

> **Action Step** — **Upon review of the statements that reflect your Ability to Trust:**

• What did you learn about yourself in regard to this attribute?

_____

_____

• How do you think your Ability to Trust influences your behavior in partnerships?

_____

_____

Future Orientation

1. I believe a person's behavior stays the same over time.

If you believe that a person's behavior doesn't change over time, you probably rely on past history to make decisions about people. This may also reflect a desire to maintain the status quo. Sometimes it's more comfortable to judge a person as "always being that way" rather than risk changing your view of them and be proven wrong.

11. I tend to make decisions about someone based on what he or she has done before.

If you make a decision based on a past event, you have a past orientation. But if you set your expectations with each individual based on the agreements you've made and then determine how well that person lives up to meeting those agreements, you have a Future Orientation.

17. Past history is a better predictor of events than a future plan.

While it is true that we can learn a lot from history, to make decisions based solely on historic data would be a mistake. People, events, and partnerships change. You certainly wouldn't drive a car while looking in the rearview mirror! It may be useful to examine where you've been and be aware of what's behind you, but it's more important to know where you're going. If you believe that past history is a better predictor of events than a future plan, you may feel uncomfortable with change and prefer the status quo.

19. I prefer to use techniques I've used before to accomplish new tasks.

If you prefer to use the same techniques on each task, you may end up making the same mistakes over and over. At the very least, you may risk missing a better way of doing things. This dynamic may also reflect your low Comfort with Change. The two dynamics often combine to create a reinforcing mechanism that is hard to break.

25. I am more interested in actualities than I am in possibilities.

People who prefer to deal with actuality rather than what may be possible can be uncomfortable making decisions based on the unknown. If this is an issue for you, you may rely more on the here-and-now rather than the future when making important decisions. You may also feel some discomfort with change. The here-and-now is tangible, and many people feel they have some control over it. Since the future is unknown, considering possibilities may cause anxiety about what changes the future may bring.

 **Action Step**   **Upon review of the statements that reflect your Future Orientation:**

• What did you learn about yourself in regard to this attribute?

_____

_____

• How do you think your Future Orientation influences your behavior in partnerships?

_____

_____

Comfort with Change

2. I like to do familiar tasks.

Maintaining the status quo means you like things as they are and do not welcome change. People who like to do familiar tasks learn how to do something and then enjoy doing it over and over. Change makes them uneasy. In partnerships, we are frequently asked to do something differently. If change makes you uncomfortable, you may find being in partnership an anxiety-ridden affair.

5. In general, I like it when everyone follows the rules.

This statement reflects on your ability to risk exploring the unknown. When people follow the rules, there is a predictability that, for some, creates comfort. Predictability reduces risk. When things are predictable, we trust that everything will turn out the way it always has in the past. Consequently, this statement posits that when we follow the rules, we maintain the status quo and know the outcome. In effect, we trust the outcome will meet our needs and expectations.

12. I feel very anxious when I'm in a new situation.

People who are uncomfortable in new situations are usually uncomfortable with change. Change can take someone out of his or her comfort zone and cause them anxiety. This statement may also reflect a need to maintain the status quo.

18. I get very nervous when I meet new people.

While meeting people for the first time can be a bit uncomfortable for some, if you get very nervous, this may indicate you have a problem with change. New people often bring unexpected challenges. If you are uncomfortable facing new challenges, meeting new people may heighten your anxiety.

27. I like having my day planned and scheduled and get frustrated when I have to change it.

Schedule changes are the norm for most of us. If schedule changes make you feel frustrated and anxious, you need to understand why. Partnerships are full of uncertainties, and if this is difficult for you, you may have a problem being in a partnership.

> **Action Step** Upon review of the statements that reflect your Comfort with Change:

• What did you learn about yourself in regard to this attribute?

_____

_____

• How do you think your level of Comfort with Change influences your behavior in partnerships?

_____

_____

Comfort with Interdependence

4. When I'm with other people, I always make sure my needs are met first.

Wanting to get your needs met first might indicate a win-lose conflict style: "I'll be sure I get mine, and we'll worry about the others later." If your needs are met first, you are less dependent on others. This statement may also reveal a lack of trust that others will help you get your needs met, creating a situation where you feel you need to "fend for yourself."

6. I like to depend on myself to get things done.

This statement reveals the level of comfort you have about being dependent on another. Frequently, when we'd rather do tasks ourselves it means we do not want to depend on someone else to help us. We may fear the "job won't get done" or that we'll be disappointed with the finished product: "If you want something done right, do it yourself." It may also indicate that we have a preferred way of doing something and that we'd rather stick to our routine.

10. I get frustrated being on a team.

When people have a strong sense of independence, teamwork is difficult for them. They dislike feeling dependent on others to achieve their goals and not being in control of the situation. If team goals are not achieved, they may blame their partners for the failure. They often would rather work by themselves because they can then trust that the job will get done.

14. When I need to go somewhere, I prefer to depend on myself to get there.

Some of us feel we "must drive ourselves," while others are willing to "share rides." This statement reflects your level of comfort in depending on others. It also involves your comfort with change and trust, since depending on another may include a "change in plans," and you must trust that others will do what they say when making arrangements.

29. I would rather be by myself than spend time with other people.

While preferring to spend time alone in itself is neither good nor bad, we all need to interact with others to get our needs met. If you are uncomfortable being with others, you might be sending your partners mixed and confusing messages. It's important to disclose to others your need for privacy or "downtime" to prevent any misunderstandings.

Action Step — **Upon review of the statements that reflect your Comfort with Interdependence:**

• What did you learn about yourself in regard to this attribute?

_____

_____

• How do you think your level of Comfort with Interdependence influences your behavior in partnerships?

_____

_____

PQ Assessment and Partnering Attribute Review

Action Step Now that you have reflected on the results of your PQ Assessment and attribute analysis, you'll want to think about how this information applies to your behaviors and experiences in partnerships by completing the exercise below.

PQ DEBRIEF

1. Do your PQ results fit with your experience? Why or why not?

_____

_____

2. What results surprised you the most?

_____

_____

3. Based on your results from the PQ Assessment and your own personal experiences in partnerships, what attributes do you consider your strengths?

_____

_____

4. Based on your results from the PQ Assessment and your own personal experiences in partnerships, what attributes do you consider your weaknesses?

_____

_____

5. How have your strengths contributed to your success in partnerships?

_____

_____

6. How have your weaknesses undermined your effectiveness in partnerships?

_____

_____

7. What insights has the PQ Assessment provided regarding your current partnerships?

_____

_____

8. Identify a currently successful partnership and list the attributes it demonstrates.

_____

_____

9. Identify a currently challenging partnership and list the attributes it does not demonstrate.

_____

_____

10. Do your professional partnerships differ from your personal partnerships? If yes, how?

_____

_____

11. Go back to the exercise on page 9 and review your answers to questions 3, 5, 6, 7, and 8. What attributes of Partnering Intelligence are being demonstrated by you and your partner? What attributes are not being demonstrated by you and your partner?

_____

_____

Action Planning

Now that you have reviewed your PQ and the nature of your partnerships, you may find it useful to take a closer look at some specific partnerships you are currently engaged in to evaluate their effectiveness and plan for needed changes to enhance them.

Action Step Think about two of your most important partnerships—one business, the other personal. Then complete the following exercise making brief notes under "Business" and "Personal." As you read the questions try to remember your strengths and weaknesses and what you have learned about your own Partnering Intelligence.

ACTION PLAN

	Business	Personal
1. Why is this partnership important to me?		
2. What are three things I need from this partnership?		
3. Why do I need to do something in this partnership?		
4. What actions do I need to take to help the partnership?		
5. What do I need to communicate to my partner?		
6. When do I need to accomplish the above actions?		
7. Who needs to be involved?		
8. How soon must I communicate with them?		
9. What tasks do the partners need to do together?		
10. What relationship activities do the partners need to take together?		
11. How will we know we are successful?		

2

Self-Disclosure and Feedback

Self-disclosure and feedback are essential skills for forming productive partnerships. From the inception of the relationship and throughout, effective two-way communication will improve the quality of the partnership and the results it produces.

The ability to provide useful feedback can be learned. While it might seem elementary, we all have mental maps regarding the sending and receiving of "sensitive" messages. Partners can work individually and together to increase their skills and comfort in these areas. This chapter will provide you with assessments and tools to build your skills and comfort level in this very important attribute for smart partnering.

The JoHari Window: A Model for Self-Disclosure and Feedback

Before we offer suggestions on how to increase your level of competency in the partnering attribute Self-Disclosure and Feedback, let's address the "Why bother?" People who find Self-Disclosure and Feedback difficult have compelling mental maps to support their beliefs about it.

Using the JoHari Window to Build Trust and Create Outstanding Results

The JoHari Window (Figure 1) derives its name from the first names of its developers, Joseph Luft and Harry Ingham. It's called a window because four "panes" are used to explain the model. The JoHari Window shows how Self-Disclosure and Feedback contributes to building trust in partnerships.

33

FIGURE 1

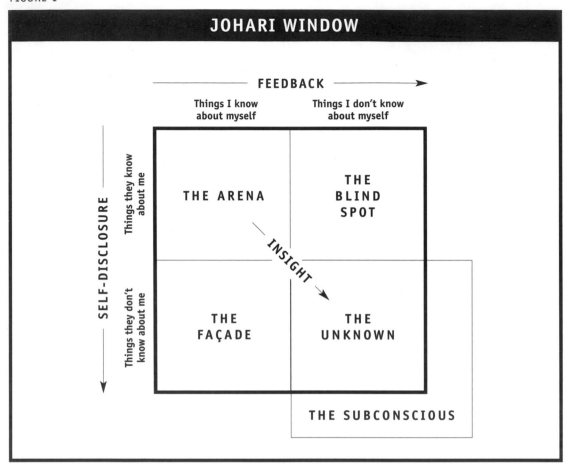

JOHARI WINDOW

→ FEEDBACK →

Things I know about myself   Things I don't know about myself

SELF-DISCLOSURE

Things they know about me

Things they don't know about me

THE ARENA

THE BLIND SPOT

INSIGHT

THE FAÇADE

THE UNKNOWN

THE SUBCONSCIOUS

Each of the panes depicts the extent to which you know yourself and your partner knows you. This information can include facts about your personal and professional lives, feelings, motivators, strengths, weaknesses, likes, dislikes, needs, values, characteristics, traits, preferences, and anything else that is part of who you are and how you behave.

The Arena represents what you know about yourself and what your partner knows about you. The Façade represents things you know about yourself that your partner does not know. The Blind Spot is information your partner has about you that you do not have. The Unknown represents information unknown to both of you but available to discovery through Self-Disclosure and Feedback. The Subconscious refers to information unavailable to both of you; therefore, the model focuses on the first four panes.

The Arena

The JoHari Window demonstrates the value of increasing the size of the Arena. The most productive partnerships have large Arenas where a great deal of information is passed back and forth. This open exchange of information is important for building trust and working creatively to achieve the best possible results.

The more you and your partner know about each other, the more likely you are to be open and creative with each another. Another dynamic that accounts for the value of a large Arena is how and where energy is focused. When you withhold information, it requires energy. When you focus energy on *not* doing something, you limit your ability to focus energy on the requirements of the partnership.

If you are uncomfortable with Self-Disclosure and Feedback, we suggest that in the beginning you share information as it relates to the tasks and outcomes of the partnership. As trust builds, we recommend expanding the information you share. For example, if you are meeting with your partner and are concerned about something in your personal life, unless you share that concern, you will be unable to focus on the purpose of the meeting. As partnerships continue over time, it becomes more and more necessary to disclose personal information to achieve the best possible outcomes.

The Façade

We all have information about ourselves that we would prefer other people did not know. It might concern our weaknesses, mistakes we have made in the past, our fears, or a broad range of other topics.

Our Façade impacts our partnerships in two ways. First, as in the Arena, withholding information takes energy that could otherwise be directed to the outcomes of the partnership. Second, our Façade can actually impact the dynamics of the partnership.

Nigel, for example, felt that he lacked skills in creating spreadsheets and was embarrassed and unwilling to disclose this to his partner, Larinda. Every time a situation arose requiring the creation of a spreadsheet, he would close down and find some excuse for Larinda to do it. Larinda didn't understand his behavior and began to think he was reluctant to do his share. Nigel sensed that Larinda was upset about something but he had no idea what it was. Eventually he came to resent her playing the martyr.

All of this could have been avoided if Nigel had disclosed his weakness to Larinda in the first place. They could have then decided that Larinda would do all the spreadsheets and Nigel would take on other tasks, or that

Nigel would use this as an opportunity to build his skill in that area with Larinda's help.

The Blind Spot

Beware of your Blind Spot! Your Blind Spot represents information that others have that you do not. What you don't know *can* hurt you!

Our experience of ourselves can be quite different from how others perceive and interpret our behavior. In our families, social and civic groups, and professional organizations, perception is reality. Unless we receive constant and accurate feedback about the perceptions of others, we might be quite unaware of what "the word" is about us.

For example, Kim was a bright but shy, soft-spoken engineer. His introversion made him uncomfortable speaking in groups. When appointed to a task force to assess the viability of a new manufacturing procedure, he was uncomfortable and quiet during the meetings.

Others on the task force were aware of how bright Kim was and interpreted his behavior to mean he felt "above it all." Thus while Kim was experiencing shyness and fear, others were defining him as "arrogant." His own experience, however, provided no information to that effect. As a result, Kim was labeled a "nonparticipant, unwilling to be a team player," which would later impact his career. Without feedback Kim could not correct this false perception because he wasn't even aware of it.

Partnerships can provide an excellent source of feedback. We will talk more about giving and receiving feedback later in this chapter.

The Unknown

The Unknown represents information that neither you nor your partner has about yourself. As Self-Disclosure and Feedback increases, the Arena becomes larger. As the Arena grows and trust builds, the opportunity to gain insights into the Unknown increases.

Assessing Comfort with Self-Disclosure

Action Step To gain a sense of your comfort level in sharing information with others, complete the Comfort with Self-Disclosure Assessment on the following pages.

COMFORT WITH SELF-DISCLOSURE ASSESSMENT

- **The Comfort with Self-Disclosure Assessment is not a test with right or wrong answers.** It is a way to get an accurate portrayal of your tendencies when it comes to sharing information with others. It is designed to be a tool to help you understand your attitudes and beliefs about self-disclosure.

- **The Comfort with Self-Disclosure Assessment is descriptive, not evaluative.** It describes your beliefs, attitudes, and orientation toward self-disclosure. The instrument itself is not meant to evaluate those beliefs, attitudes, or orientation. Rather, it helps you to understand how you disclose information about yourself in partnerships.

Directions

- Circle the choice—*a, b,* or *c*—that describes you best.

- Do not contemplate a statement too long. Your initial response is likely to be the most accurate one.

- Rate the statements as honestly as you can. The extent to which this tool is useful depends on how accurately it reflects what is actually true for you.

1. When I have strong feelings about something:

a. I make them known to most people.

b. I keep them to myself.

c. I tell others only if I feel close to them.

2. If I have a squabble with a family member, I will:

a. Keep it to myself, because it's no one's business but ours.

b. Discuss it with a close friend just to get another perspective.

c. Tell anyone as long as I neither cause any harm to the family member nor betray any confidences.

3. In business situations, over time:

a. I reveal a lot about my personal life to people I feel close to.

b. I reveal a lot about my personal life to most people I work with.

c. I reveal only "surface" information about my personal life, such as activities or events that I enjoy.

4. Others would say that:

a. I am easy to get to know.

b. I am difficult to get to know.

c. Neither of the above.

5. If someone I work with does something I don't like:

a. I will put up with it as long as I can and then tell them.

b. I will tell them immediately and ask them to change their behavior in the future.

c. I will not tell them for fear of hurting their feelings or damaging the relationship.

6. When meeting someone for the first time at a business conference:

a. I feel comfortable sharing any information about my personal life.

b. I share very little or only "surface" information about my personal life.

c. I will share information about my personal life if I "click" with the person.

7. If I am proud of something I accomplish:

a. I will not tell anyone for fear of bragging.

b. I will tell only those people who are close to me.

c. I will tell everyone.

8. In relationships:

a. I withhold information if I think it will be embarrassing or uncomfortable for my partner or for me to share it.

b. I share "sensitive" information only when absolutely necessary.

c. I usually don't withhold any information unless it is hurtful and unnecessary to share.

9. When it comes to emotions:

a. I find it easy to share them with others.

b. I tend to keep them to myself.

c. I share them only with people close to me.

10. If I want something from another person:

a. I am usually hesitant to ask.

b. I find it easy to ask for it.

c. I try to get a sense of how they might receive my request before I ask for what I want.

11. Others would say that:

a. They always know how I think and feel about most things.

b. They know what I think and feel about some things, but I tend to keep sensitive issues to myself.

c. They rarely know what I am thinking or feeling.

12. If I ask another person to do something and they give me something other than what I wanted:

a. I will try to make it work and tell them only if I have to.

b. I will try to make it work and do it over myself if I cannot.

c. Thank them and explain that I had something different in mind.

13. For the most part, when I am unhappy with someone:

a. I will tell them even if it might upset them.

b. I will tell them if I am sure it will not upset them.

c. I will tell them only if absolutely necessary.

14. If someone asks me a question about a sensitive topic:

a. I evade the question.

b. I answer the question briefly, giving as little information as possible.

c. I answer the question fully.

15. Others would describe me as a person:

a. Who plays their cards very close to the vest.

b. Whose life is an open book.

c. Neither of the above.

16. If I fail to accomplish something:

a. I say so.

b. I try not to say anything to anyone.

c. I tell people if I absolutely have to.

17. When dealing with most people:

a. I wait a while before I reveal much about my personal life.

b. I am open about my personal life from the beginning.

c. I am careful not to reveal things about my personal life.

18. The following statement is the most true for me:

a. I don't care what people know about me.

b. I am most comfortable when I can choose what people know about me.

c. I would prefer that people know only what they have to about me.

19. In a work situation:

a. I believe that information is power and prefer to keep it to myself.

b. I openly share information.

c. I share information on a "need to know" basis.

20. If I do not get something that I have worked hard to achieve:

a. I don't care who knows it.

b. I don't want anyone to know.

c. I want only my close friends to know.

Assessment Score Sheet

Tally your numerical score for each item and enter it in the space provided. Then add up your scores and enter the total score at the bottom.

1. a = 3 points	b = 1 point	c = 2 points	Points on #1	_____
2. a = 1 point	b = 2 points	c = 3 points	Points on #2	_____
3. a = 2 points	b = 3 points	c = 1 point	Points on #3	_____
4. a = 3 points	b = 1 point	c = 2 points	Points on #4	_____
5. a = 2 points	b = 3 points	c = 1 point	Points on #5	_____
6. a = 3 points	b = 1 point	c = 2 points	Points on #6	_____
7. a = 1 point	b = 2 points	c = 3 points	Points on #7	_____
8. a = 2 points	b = 1 point	c = 3 points	Points on #8	_____
9. a = 3 points	b = 1 point	c = 2 points	Points on #9	_____
10. a = 1 point	b = 3 points	c = 2 points	Points on #10	_____
11. a = 3 points	b = 2 points	c = 1 point	Points on #11	_____
12. a = 2 points	b = 1 point	c = 3 points	Points on #12	_____
13. a = 3 points	b = 2 points	c = 1 point	Points on #13	_____
14. a = 1 point	b = 2 points	c = 3 points	Points on #14	_____
15. a = 1 point	b = 3 points	c = 2 points	Points on #15	_____
16. a = 3 points	b = 1 point	c = 2 points	Points on #16	_____
17. a = 2 points	b = 3 points	c = 1 point	Points on #17	_____
18. a = 3 points	b = 2 points	c = 1 point	Points on #18	_____
19. a = 1 point	b = 3 points	c = 2 points	Points on #19	_____
20. a = 3 points	b = 1 point	c = 2 points	Points on #20	_____

Total Score _____

Interpreting Your Assessment Score

Your comfort with self-disclosure forms a continuum rather than distinct categories. The higher your score, the more comfortable you are providing others with information about yourself. The lower your score, the more difficult you find it to tell others about yourself.

Action Step Compare the total score you entered on your score sheet with the scoring ranges below. Then proceed with the interpretive information that follows.

Understanding Your Total Score

50–60 Points: High comfort level with self-disclosure

40–49 Points: High–moderate comfort level with self-disclosure

30–39 Points: Low–moderate comfort level with self-disclosure

20–29 Points: Low comfort level with self-disclosure

If you scored high on this attribute (50–60 points), you are an open person who discloses information and feelings quite easily. Others always know where you stand and how you feel, and they feel as if they know you well both personally and professionally. You ask for what you want and tell it like it is.

Your effect on others is usually one that encourages them, in turn, to share information about themselves with you. When you are open about your fallibility, idiosyncrasies, and disappointments, others feel comfortable that you won't judge them if they reveal theirs.

If you scored high–moderate on this attribute (40–49 points), you are fairly comfortable providing others with information about yourself. You tell them what you need to in order to get your needs met and accomplish joint ventures.

If you scored low–moderate on this attribute (30–39 points), it is more challenging for you to self-disclose. There are circumstances where you might sacrifice getting your needs met. You may tend to feel uncomfortable in, and sometimes avoid, situations that require you to provide sensitive information.

If you scored low on this attribute (20–29 points), you will usually withhold information. You tend to have difficulties in partnerships when self-disclosure becomes necessary. You must be careful that you don't forgo the opportunity to get your needs met or create high-quality results due to your reluctance to speak up. You must also guard against eventual resentment because you are not getting what you need or want from the partnership.

Increasing Your Ability to Self-Disclose

Please note that this section is not titled "Increasing Your *Comfort with* Self-Disclosure." The lower your score, the more challenging this attribute is for you. However, when necessary to the success of a partnership, you can change your behavior and self-disclose even if it feels uncomfortable. If self-disclosure does not come naturally to you, the first step to take is to identify your individual needs and what your partner needs to know to help you fulfill those needs.

It is true that sometimes our mental maps make self-disclosure risky. Common themes are fears of rejection, criticism, vulnerability, and loss of, or damage to, relationships. Whatever your beliefs, failure to share information as it relates to a partnership can ultimately damage the relationship.

Action Step **Think about a partnership you are currently engaged in and identify the information that needs to be conveyed to your partner. Then complete the following exercise to help you decide if it is worth it to you to offer this information. You will want to ask yourself:**

1. What information does my partner need in order for me to receive what I need from this partnership?

2. What are the risks in revealing this information?

3. What are the rewards or possible gains if I reveal this information?

Write short answers to questions 1–3 in the first three columns to help you decide if self-disclosure is worth the risk; then circle "yes" or "no" in the right-hand column.

RISK/REWARD ANALYSIS			
Information	Risks	Rewards	Worth the Risk?
			Yes No
			Yes No
			Yes No

Assessing Comfort with Giving Feedback

Giving feedback in a partnership takes self-disclosure to another dimension. It requires that you provide information about another person's effect on you and/or others.

Action Step To help you determine your comfort level with the important communication skill of giving feedback, which requires you to be forthright with your own feelings and impressions, complete the assessment on the following pages.

COMFORT WITH GIVING FEEDBACK ASSESSMENT

Directions

- For the situations described below, note which action you are most likely to take—*a*, *b*, or *c*—by entering the letter in the space to the right of each statement.

a = Initiate a request to offer feedback on what I'm thinking, feeling, and/or observing

b = Wait until I've been asked what I am thinking, feeling, and/or observing

c = Refrain from saying what I am thinking, feeling, and/or observing even if asked

- Do not contemplate a statement too long. Your initial response is likely to be the most accurate one.

- Rate the statements as honestly as you can. The extent to which this tool is useful depends on how accurately it reflects what is actually true for you.

Statement	Action
1. I am having dinner with a co-worker, and he has food on his chin.	
2. I am upset that a friend is not including me in the planning of a surprise party for someone I am close to.	
3. I think my partner handled a delicate situation exceptionally well.	
4. I think my partner could prepare more detailed customer reports.	
5. A co-worker makes a comment that offends me.	
6. I am with a friend who is purchasing new stereo speakers and I think the quality of his selection is not comparable to the rest of his system.	
7. I admire my partner for his project management skills.	
8. A partner is continually late, and I could be putting the time spent waiting for her to better use.	
9. I am dissatisfied with the quality of a team member's work on a project.	
10. I think my partner did an exceptional job on a marketing presentation.	

Statement	Action
11. My peer is perceived by her direct reports to be micromanaging.	
12. I feel that a co-worker is not doing his share on a joint project.	
13. I disagree with the project lead's assessment that a piece of work is of sufficient quality.	
14. I feel that I could not have succeeded without my partner's input.	
15. I notice someone getting into a car that has a low rear tire.	
16. I keep getting interrupted by a colleague when I'm trying to finish an important project.	
17. I think the presentation my partner developed could be improved.	
18. A friend is telling me about an argument he had with a co-worker, and I think he was the one in the wrong.	
19. My partner is presenting to an important customer and has not prepared overheads, which I think are very important.	
20. I think my partner's listening skills are exceptional.	

Assessment Score Sheet

The point value of your answer for each statement is as follows:

a = 3 points   **b** = 2 points   **c** = 1 point

Tally your numerical score for each item and enter it in the space provided. Then add up your scores and enter the total score at the bottom.

1. _____	6. _____	11. _____	16. _____
2. _____	7. _____	12. _____	17. _____
3. _____	8. _____	13. _____	18. _____
4. _____	9. _____	14. _____	19. _____
5. _____	10. _____	15. _____	20. _____

Total Score _____

Interpreting Your Assessment Score

Your comfort with giving feedback forms a continuum. The higher your score, the more comfortable you are providing feedback. The lower your score, the more difficult it is for you.

Action Step Compare the total score you entered on your score sheet with the scoring ranges below. Then proceed with the interpretive information that follows.

Understanding Your Total Score

50–60 Points: High comfort level with giving feedback

40–49 Points: High–moderate comfort level with giving feedback

30–39 Points: Low–moderate comfort level with giving feedback

20–29 Points: Low comfort level with giving feedback

There are several ways to use your score to better understand your comfort with giving feedback and to increase your ability to do so in partnerships. Further, the Comfort with Giving Feedback Assessment can be a means for you to discover what mental maps and beliefs influence your willingness to give feedback in each of the following four categories:

• **Category 1:** Feedback offered only for the benefit of the recipient, with no stake in any action being taken on your part

• **Category 2:** Feedback on behavior or actions you'd like the recipient to change

• **Category 3:** Feedback offered on the quality of what someone produces because you want the recipient to improve upon those products or outcomes

• **Category 4:** Feedback offered to praise behavior or outcomes that you want the recipient to continue

Usually we are hesitant to give feedback because of a belief that it represents risk. If you are aware of your beliefs and what you feel you might be risking by giving feedback, you can consciously decide to take the risk.

EXAMPLE STATEMENTS:

- "I believe that if you can't say something nice, you shouldn't say anything at all; therefore, I don't want to risk people perceiving that I'm not a nice person."

- "I believe that people get angry when they hear something they don't like; therefore, I don't want to risk having someone get mad at me."

- "I believe people should mind their own business; therefore, I don't want to risk offending someone."

> **Action Step** Now complete the assessment on the following pages to help you determine your comfort level in giving feedback in each of the four categories just outlined. Begin by thinking about what the perceived risks are that prevent you from giving feedback.

COMFORT WITH GIVING FEEDBACK RISK ASSESSMENT

Directions

From the Comfort with Giving Feedback Assessment score sheet on page 47, transfer your scores—1, 2, or 3—to each of the following four categories to evaluate your beliefs and perceived risks in giving feedback.

Category 1: Feedback offered only for the benefit of the recipient, with no stake in any action being taken on your part

Your scores on statements in the assessment that fall in this category:

Statement 1 _____   Statement 11 _____   Statement 18 _____

Statement 6 _____   Statement 15 _____

For each statement above that you rated as a "2" or a "1," complete the following sentence:

- I answered Statement # _____ the way I did because I believe that: _____

  _____

  and therefore did not want to risk: _____

- I answered Statement # _____ the way I did because I believe that: _____

  _____

  and therefore did not want to risk: _____

- I answered Statement # _____ the way I did because I believe that: _____

  _____

  and therefore did not want to risk: _____

- I answered Statement # _____ the way I did because I believe that: _____

  _____

  and therefore did not want to risk: _____

- I answered Statement # _____ the way I did because I believe that: _____

  _____

  and therefore did not want to risk: _____

Category 2: Feedback on behavior or actions you'd like the recipient to change

Your scores on statements in the assessment that fall in this category:

Statement 2 _____   Statement 8 _____   Statement 16 _____

Statement 5 _____   Statement 12 _____

For each statement above that you rated as a "2" or a "1," complete the following sentence:

- I answered Statement # _____ the way I did because I believe that: _____

  _____

  and therefore did not want to risk: _____

- I answered Statement # _____ the way I did because I believe that: _____

  _____

  and therefore did not want to risk: _____

- I answered Statement # _____ the way I did because I believe that: _____

  _____

  and therefore did not want to risk: _____

- I answered Statement # _____ the way I did because I believe that: _____

  _____

  and therefore did not want to risk: _____

- I answered Statement # _____ the way I did because I believe that: _____

  _____

  and therefore did not want to risk: _____

Category 3: Feedback offered on the quality of what someone produces because you want the recipient to improve upon those products or outcomes

Your scores on statements in the assessment that fall in this category:

Statement 4 _____   Statement 13 _____   Statement 19 _____

Statement 9 _____   Statement 17 _____

For each statement above that you rated as a "2" or a "1," complete the following sentence:

- I answered Statement # _____ the way I did because I believe that: _____

  _____

  and therefore did not want to risk: _____

- I answered Statement # _____ the way I did because I believe that: _____

  _____

  and therefore did not want to risk: _____

- I answered Statement # _____ the way I did because I believe that: _____

  _____

  and therefore did not want to risk: _____

- I answered Statement # _____ the way I did because I believe that: _____

  _____

  and therefore did not want to risk: _____

- I answered Statement # _____ the way I did because I believe that: _____

  _____

  and therefore did not want to risk: _____

Category 4: Feedback offered to praise behavior or outcomes that you want the recipient to continue

Your scores on statements in the assessment that fall in this category:

Statement 3 _____   Statement 10 _____   Statement 20 _____

Statement 7 _____   Statement 14 _____

For each statement above that you rated as a "2" or a "1," complete the following sentence:

- I answered Statement # _____ the way I did because I believe that: _____

  _____

  and therefore did not want to risk: _____

- I answered Statement # _____ the way I did because I believe that: _____

  _____

  and therefore did not want to risk: _____

- I answered Statement # _____ the way I did because I believe that: _____

  _____

  and therefore did not want to risk: _____

- I answered Statement # _____ the way I did because I believe that: _____

  _____

  and therefore did not want to risk: _____

- I answered Statement # _____ the way I did because I believe that: _____

  _____

  and therefore did not want to risk: _____

Action Step   Summarize briefly your beliefs about giving feedback by reviewing your responses to the risk assessment and complete the following exercise. Then continue with the next Action Step.

BELIEFS OR ASSUMPTIONS ABOUT GIVING FEEDBACK			
Beliefs	Positive Impacts of My Beliefs	Negative Impacts of My Beliefs	Needed Changes to My Beliefs

Action Step   Now consider a current partnership and take appropriate action.

1. Discuss the impact of your beliefs with your partner and gain agreement about what feedback you will offer one another.

2. Weigh the potential risk to the partnership if you do not offer the feedback versus the potential benefits if you do. Decide if you or your partner would be willing to take the risk and/or forgo the potential benefits. If you are unwilling to forgo the benefits, then you are obligated to offer the feedback in spite of the risks.

Guidelines for Giving and Receiving Feedback

The way that feedback is given or received will greatly impact a partnership. The following guidelines on giving and receiving feedback will serve as a review to many and as a useful overview to those new to the subject.

Criteria for Giving Feedback

- **It is provided for the right reasons.** Your reason for giving feedback should be either that you think your partner might want to know or you are requesting that he or she change or continue a specific behavior.

  If your intention is to be hurtful, get even, or take out your frustrations, don't disguise it as feedback! It is best to redirect your energy in this situation and refrain from saying anything at all. When we react out of a desire to hurt or to take out our problems on someone else, we undermine trust, create defensiveness, and minimize the impact of feedback that we offer in the future.

- **It is descriptive, not evaluative, and focused on a specific behavior.** You might say "you are often late" as opposed to "you are inconsiderate."

  When feedback is focused on behavior, both the giver and receiver can clearly and objectively identify what the issue is. This is true both for when you want something to change and when you want it to continue. Often people have "unconscious competence." They do not realize they are skilled at something or what it is about them that makes them skilled. "You really diffused the tension in the room when you made that comment about Charlie's tie" contains more useful information to someone with unconscious competence than the vague statement "You are so good with people."

  If you want something to change, focusing on behavior instead of evaluating that behavior allows others to actually hear the feedback and use it as they see fit, eliminating the tendency to respond defensively.

- **It is actionable.** Feedback should be directed toward behavior the receiver can do something about.

- **You offered with permission.** Either you have requested permission or the receiver has asked for feedback.

- **It is well timed.** Feedback is most useful when it is offered at the earliest opportunity after the behavior has occurred.

Make an exception when either your own or the receiver's emotions need to be considered. If you are feeling angry or resentful, your feelings will be communicated nonverbally and will interfere with the usefulness of the feedback no matter what words you choose. You might want to "cool off" before offering the feedback to avoid putting the receiver on the defensive. If the receiver is upset or emotional about his or her behavior that might have contributed to the outcome, it is best to wait until just prior to when the person is likely to repeat the behavior.

- **It is a suggestion, rather than an imperative demand.**

- **It is presented a little at a time.** Too much feedback is overwhelming and not useful to the recipient.

Criteria for Receiving Feedback

- **Request to receive feedback or give permission for it.** Feedback is essential to our understanding of how we impact others and how what we produce is received.

  Often our experience of ourselves or of what we produce differs from how we are perceived by others. If we are not aware of those perceptions, this can seriously influence whether we get what we want from our professional and personal lives.

- **Listen without becoming defensive or emotional.** If people have to defend their feedback or deal with your emotional response to it, they are less likely to offer feedback in the future.

- **Ask questions for clarification only.** If the feedback is offered without malice, it is always true for the giver. It does not mean that it is true for others or that you have to act on it.

  Make sure you understand what the giver wants to communicate. In order to determine whether the feedback is true for others or if you want to act on it, you must be sure that you understand it.

- **Acknowledge the feedback.** Thank the giver for his or her feedback.

- **Reflect on the value of the feedback and on whether you wish to act on it.** You might decide not to act on feedback if, when you talk to others, you find that the feedback was the result of an idiosyncrasy of the giver. You might also decide that changing a particular behavior or result is not a priority for you.

Win-Win Orientation

Successful partnerships require that all parties feel that their needs are being met and that they are gaining something from the relationship. A Win-Win Orientation is essential for all partners to contribute their best and thus achieve the greatest possible results. A Win-Win Orientation is a problem-solving and conflict resolution strategy that ensures that everyone involved feels that they win.

Assessing Orientation to Problem-Solving and Conflict Resolution

Action Step The first step toward a Win-Win Orientation is to understand your personal approach to problem solving and conflict resolution. Complete the following assessment to help you determine your current style and provide a basis for increasing your skill at reaching win-win outcomes.

WIN-WIN ORIENTATION ASSESSMENT

- **The Win-Win Orientation Assessment is not a test with right or wrong answers.** It is a way to get an accurate portrayal of your strengths and weaknesses in working toward win-win outcomes. It is designed to help you increase your skill in this important partnering attribute.

- **The Win-Win Orientation Assessment is descriptive, not evaluative.** This assessment describes your beliefs, attitudes, and orientation toward achieving win-win outcomes. The instrument itself is not meant to evaluate those beliefs, attitudes, or orientation. Rather, it provides you with a profile that you can use in current or future relationships to enhance your effectiveness.

Directions

- Use the following scale to score each statement:

  1 = Strongly Agree
  2 = Agree
  3 = Somewhat Agree
  4 = Somewhat Disagree
  5 = Disagree
  6 = Strongly Disagree

- Enter your score in the shaded box to the right of each statement.

- Pick a context from which to respond to the survey, either your work life or home life. Think about how you would typically react in the situation described in the statement. Do not contemplate a statement too long. Your initial response is likely to be the most accurate one.

- Score the statements as honestly as you can. The extent to which this tool is useful depends upon how accurately it reflects what is actually true for you.

1 = Strongly Agree   2 = Agree   3 = Somewhat Agree   4 = Somewhat Disagree   5 = Disagree   6 = Strongly Disagree

Statement	A	B	C	D	E
1. I don't give up until the other person agrees with me.				X	
2. I'd rather fix half the problem than make no progress at all.			X		
3. I try to make everyone around me happy.			X		
4. I cooperate with others to help them achieve their goals.					X
5. When others are having problems, I mind my own business.	X				
6. I move others to the middle ground.			X		
7. I can adjust to any situation and feel good.	X				
8. When I know I'm right about a problem, I work hard to convince others to see it my way.				X	
9. I give in to others to keep the peace.	X				
10. When fixing a problem, it's important that people get what they want.					X
11. In problem solving, I will generally "go with the flow" to make things easy.		X			
12. I try to reach consensus on issues between people.				X	
13. I get nervous when confronting problems.	X				
14. Conflict is good because it separates the winners from the losers.				X	
15. I feel good when we've reached a compromise.			X		
16. It is important to me to avoid arguments.	X				
17. When there is a problem, I want to fix it my way.				X	
18. Giving in to another's solution is all right as long as some of my needs are met.			X		
19. It is important to make people comfortable, so I oblige when solving problems.		X			
20. I am uncomfortable when people argue over the issues.	X				
Subtotal					

WIN-WIN ORIENTATION ASSESSMENT (CONTINUED)

1 = Strongly Agree   2 = Agree   3 = Somewhat Agree   4 = Somewhat Disagree   5 = Disagree   6 = Strongly Disagree

Statement	A	B	C	D	E
21. When solving a problem, I am not satisfied until everyone involved agrees with the solution.					■
22. I know what I want and I pursue it.				■	
23. Other people's feelings are important to me.		■			
24. I will give up something to move ahead.			■		
25. I avoid conflict if I can.	■				
26. When I am responsible for a problem, I want control over how to fix it.				■	
27. I talk about problems and ask for others' thoughts.					■
28. I feel best when everyone wins.					■
29. I believe it's better to give up something than to lose everything.		■			
30. I feel harmony is more important than meeting my needs.	■				
31. If there is a problem, I tend to look the other way.	■				
32. Even if a problem is important to me, I pride myself on adapting to any solution.		■			
33. I am concerned about what others need.					■
34. I seek to find a solution even if it means making concessions.			■		
35. I will not talk about an issue if I think it will create a problem.		■			
36. I will push to get my way if I think I am right.				■	
37. I think it is important to give up something if it keeps the peace.			■		
38. When people are arguing over how to solve a problem, I stay out of it.	■				
39. I get upset when I lose on an issue.				■	
40. I think it is important to discuss the issues and identify needs with everyone before solving the problem.					■
Subtotal					

Assessment Score Sheet

Subtotal your scores at the bottom of each column on pages 59 and 60 by adding up the numbers in the shaded boxes. Next, combine the subtotals here and transfer the total scores to the Win-Win Orientation Assessment Grid on the following page.

Column A: Subtotal (page 59)   _____
                Subtotal (page 60)   _____

                    Total Score   _____

Column B: Subtotal (page 59)   _____
                Subtotal (page 60)   _____

                    Total Score   _____

Column C: Subtotal (page 59)   _____
                Subtotal (page 60)   _____

                    Total Score   _____

Column D: Subtotal (page 59)   _____
                Subtotal (page 60)   _____

                    Total Score   _____

Column E: Subtotal (page 59)   _____
                Subtotal (page 60)   _____

                    Total Score   _____

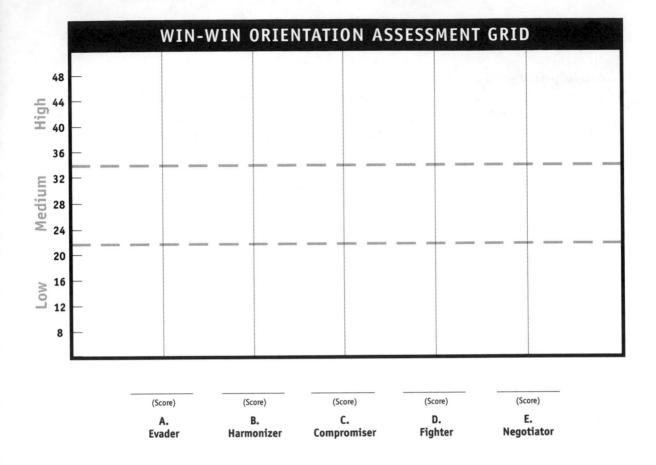

WIN-WIN ORIENTATION ASSESSMENT GRID

	(Score)	(Score)	(Score)	(Score)	(Score)
	A. Evader	**B.** Harmonizer	**C.** Compromiser	**D.** Fighter	**E.** Negotiator

Plot your individual scores on the appropriate vertical line. Continue until all five columns have been graphed. Then, connect the points with a line.

Note that each column is labeled with an indicator of problem-solving style, to be discussed in detail on the following pages. For now, simply note your problem-solving style preferences based on the following scoring key:

- **High (34–48 points)** indicates a strong preference for that style, which is one you probably use frequently

- **Medium (22–33 points)** indicates an occasional preference for that style, which you probably use in a specific type of situation

- **Low (8–21 points)** represents a style that you rarely, if ever, use—one that you probably resort to only under extreme circumstances

It is important that you understand your preferred styles and your partners' preferred styles in solving problems and resolving conflicts. This awareness provides a base for discussion and sets the stage for moving toward a Win-Win Orientation.

Problem-Solving and Conflict Resolution Styles

The strategies you use to resolve task-related problems and interpersonal conflicts require the same sets of skills. Regardless of the nature of the problem, when the situation involves more than one person, using your Partnering Intelligence to satisfy the needs of all is critical to the ultimate success of any partnering endeavor. This is easy when all partners have similar objectives and needs. When the objectives and needs of the partners are not mutually compatible, greater effort is required to create a win-win outcome.

Partnerships are formed to fulfill individual needs. How we get needs met is a critical part of creating successful partnerships. The individual styles of the partners in their approach to problem solving influence the extent to which the partnership is able to create outcomes that meet the needs of all.

Our styles often indicate underlying beliefs we have about getting our needs met and about problems and conflict in general. The higher the score on a style, the stronger our underlying beliefs and the greater the risk in deviating from that style.

As noted on the Win-Win Orientation Assessment Grid, there are five basic styles or approaches to problem solving and conflict resolution: Evader, Harmonizer, Compromiser, Fighter, and Negotiator. These are shown in Figure 2 on the next page and are described in detail in the pages that follow.

FIGURE 2

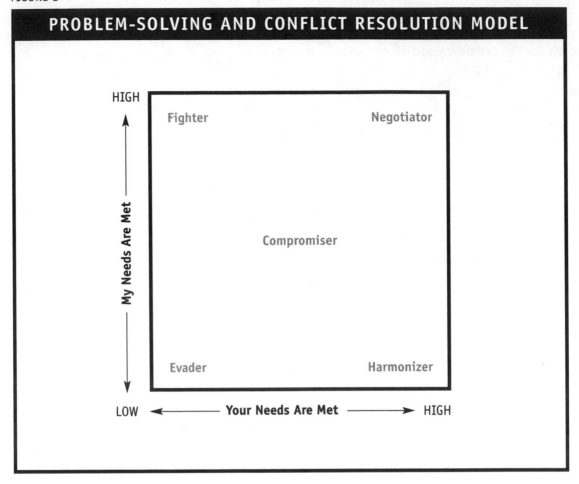

PROBLEM-SOLVING AND CONFLICT RESOLUTION MODEL

The Evader

Evaders avoid facing problems. They would rather not be forced into a situation where they feel uncomfortable or under stress. Evaders do not have a high desire to get their needs meet. They would rather sacrifice their own needs than confront issues that may be difficult or uncomfortable to resolve.

KEY WORD DESCRIPTORS

Shun, stay away from, refrain from, abstain from, circumvent, ward off, fend off, flee from, shrink from, elude, recoil from, let alone, yield to, submit to, be passive.

SAMPLE OF UNDERLYING BELIEFS AND LANGUAGE

- Conflict is dangerous; therefore, "It really isn't such a big deal if Mary takes over the marketing plan."

- People get hurt in arguments; therefore, "It isn't worth it to confront Sam about what he said at the party last night."

- Conflict means that there is something wrong or bad; therefore, "Sue and I have been working so well together—I don't want to ruin it by pushing back about who will run the meeting."

- I'm not very good at getting my needs met; therefore, "It will only cause problems if I bring up the work assignments, and it probably won't change anything anyway."

- I don't deserve to get my needs met; therefore, "I won't say anything about wanting to manage the project, because Sally is really very competent and has been here longer than I have."

IMPACT

When one partner evades, or refuses to deal with, issues, both partners lose the ability to share insights and solutions that might help them get their needs met. The Evader style allows one party to dominate the partnership, depriving the partnership of its potential by limiting information and problem solving to one-sided input.

OUTCOME

Lose-lose.

STATEMENTS THAT CHARACTERIZE THE EVADER STYLE (SEE PAGES 59–60)

5. When others are having problems, I mind my own business.
13. I get nervous when confronting problems.
16. It is important to me to avoid arguments.
20. I am uncomfortable when people argue over the issues.
25. I avoid conflict if I can.
31. If there is a problem, I tend to look the other way.
35. I will not talk about an issue if I think it will create a problem.
38. When people are arguing over how to solve a problem, I stay out of it.

EXAMINING YOUR SCORE

Action Step Referring to the Win-Win Orientation Assessment Grid on page 62, indicate your scoring range for the Evader style and answer the questions below.

High _____   Medium _____   Low _____

If you scored in the high or medium range, think of a recent situation in which you behaved as an Evader.

What was the situation?

_____

What beliefs supported your behaviors?

_____

What were the risks you wanted to avoid?

_____

What might you have done differently?

_____

What would have been the value derived from doing things differently?

_____

The Harmonizer

STYLE DESCRIPTION

Harmonizers value peace at any cost, and they are willing to sacrifice their needs and those of others toward that end. Harmonizers will quickly give in to others the moment they feel that to do otherwise might "cause a problem."

Harmonizers will help their partners get their needs met at the expense of their own. Often people will describe Harmonizers as "easy to get along with" or "generous and flexible."

KEY WORD DESCRIPTORS

Accommodate, adapt to, adjust to, acclimate to, get used to, oblige, make comfortable, please, gratify, indulge.

SAMPLE OF UNDERLYING BELIEFS AND LANGUAGE

Harmonizers and Evaders share similar beliefs that cause them both to dislike conflict. The difference between the two is that an Evader won't engage at all in exploring needs for fear of confrontation, whereas a Harmonizer will engage in such a conversation but back down immediately to avoid conflict. In addition to sharing the beliefs of an Evader, a Harmonizer might think the following:

- People won't like me unless I accommodate them; therefore, "Jim's good will is worth more than how we design the project."

- Relationships dissolve when there is disagreement; therefore, "It's just not worth it to tell Max that I don't agree with his projections."

- Confrontation can lead to permanent ill will between people; therefore, "I value Sara's friendship too much to argue about who's invited to the party."

IMPACT

When the Harmonizer gives in and sacrifices what he or she needs, the stage is set for resentment down the road, which will be acted out in passive-aggressive behaviors.

OUTCOME

Lose-win.

STATEMENTS THAT CHARACTERIZE THE HARMONIZER STYLE (SEE PAGES 59–60)

3. I try to make everyone around me happy.

7. I can adjust to any situation and feel good.

9. I give in to others to keep the peace.

11. In problem solving, I will generally "go with the flow" to make things easy.

19. It is important to make people comfortable, so I oblige them when solving problems.

23. Other people's feelings are important to me.

30. I feel harmony is more important than meeting my needs.

32. Even if a problem is important to me, I pride myself on adapting to any solution.

EXAMINING YOUR SCORE

Action Step   **Referring to the Win-Win Orientation Assessment Grid on page 62, indicate your scoring range for the Harmonizer style and answer the questions below.**

High _____   Medium _____   Low _____

If you scored in the high or medium range, think of a recent situation in which you behaved as a Harmonizer.

What was the situation?

_____

What beliefs supported your behaviors?

_____

What were the risks you wanted to avoid?

_____

What might you have done differently?

_____

What would have been the value derived from doing things differently?

The Compromiser

STYLE DESCRIPTION

Compromisers will assert their needs up to a point. As the obstacles mount, however, they are willing to give up something important to meet other partners halfway—and they expect the other partners to do the same. Rather than work through issues, Compromisers look at what each party is willing to give up in order to "meet in the middle."

KEY WORD DESCRIPTORS

Mutual concessions, conciliation, giving up, intermediate position, halfway.

SAMPLE OF UNDERLYING BELIEFS AND LANGUAGE

- Nothing is ever perfect; therefore, "We should figure out how to make the best of this—I'll give up tennis if you give up choir."

- Compromise is the best way to solve problems; therefore, "I'll concede the project lead if you agree to slowing down the timeline."

- It isn't right to be greedy or self-promoting; therefore, "I'm willing to be reasonable and give up my need for quiet time if we watch the program I want on television."

- I can't always have things my way; therefore, "I can manage without administrative support if you let me use your laptop."

- No one ever wins when there is conflict; therefore, "We both have to give a little."

IMPACT

Compromisers essentially set up lose-lose situations where all parties give up something in order to make a solution acceptable. Everyone loses equally as opposed to everyone winning. Ultimately the partnership cannot reach its full potential.

OUTCOME

Lose-lose.

STATEMENTS THAT CHARACTERIZE THE COMPROMISER STYLE (SEE PAGES 59–60)

2. I'd rather fix half the problem than make no progress at all.
6. I move others to the middle ground.
15. I feel good when we've reached a compromise.
18. Giving in to another's solution is all right as long as some of my needs are met.
24. I will give up something to move ahead.
29. I believe it's better to give up something than to lose everything.
34. I seek to find a solution even if it means making concessions.
37. I think it is important to give up something if it keeps the peace.

EXAMINING YOUR SCORE

Action Step **Referring to the Win-Win Orientation Assessment Grid on page 62, indicate your scoring range for the Compromiser style and answer the questions below.**

High _____   Medium _____   Low _____

If you scored in the high or medium range, think of a recent situation in which you behaved as a Compromiser.

What was the situation?

_____

What beliefs supported your behaviors?

_____

What were the risks you wanted to avoid?

_____

What might you have done differently?

_____

What would have been the value derived from doing things differently?

_____

The Fighter

STYLE DESCRIPTION

Fighters turn every problem or conflict into a contest that they must win. They assert their needs and intend to meet them at the expense of anyone else involved. For them, the key issue is to win.

KEY WORD DESCRIPTORS

Adversary, antagonist, contestant, battle, fight, rival, contender, combatant, challenger, competitor.

SAMPLE OF UNDERLYING BELIEFS AND LANGUAGE

- In order for me to win, someone else has to lose; therefore, "I will drop out of the project unless we do things the way I say."

- I have to fight to get what I want; therefore, "I will do whatever it takes to make sure I get credit for winning that client."

- You've got to look out for number one; therefore, "I'll make absolutely sure I always get what I need."

- Winning is more important than anything else; therefore, "I will win this argument at any price."

IMPACT

When the Fighter style is predominant, partners will engage in a contest each time an issue arises. Being right becomes the focus of discussions as opposed to what is best for everyone. Trust is eroded every time a problem turns into a situation where someone must lose. Ultimately the partnership is placed in jeopardy.

OUTCOME

Win-lose.

STATEMENTS THAT CHARACTERIZE THE FIGHTER STYLE (SEE PAGES 59–60)

1. I don't give up until the other person agrees with me.
8. When I know I'm right about a problem, I work hard to convince others to see it my way.
14. Conflict is good because it separates the winners from the losers.
17. When there is a problem, I want to fix it my way.
22. I know what I want and I pursue it.
26. When I am responsible for a problem, I want control over how to fix it.
36. I will push to get my way if I think I am right.
39. I get upset when I lose on an issue.

EXAMINING YOUR SCORE

Action Step Referring to the Win-Win Orientation Assessment Grid on page 62, indicate your scoring range for the Fighter style and answer the questions below.

High _____   Medium _____   Low _____

If you scored in the high or medium range, think of a recent situation in which you behaved as a Fighter.

What was the situation?

_____

What beliefs supported your behaviors?

_____

What were the risks you wanted to avoid?

_____

What might you have done differently?

_____

What would have been the value derived from doing things differently?

_____

The Negotiator

STYLE DESCRIPTION

Negotiators approach problems and conflicts by identifying the issues and underlying needs that are important to those involved. They then begin searching for solutions that meet those needs while solving the problem. They continue to seek more information about the problem while keeping the lines of communication open. By continually seeking more information, they discover more options to address the problem until everyone involved feels their needs have been addressed.

KEY WORD DESCRIPTORS

Collaborate, disclose, ask for feedback, team up with, work jointly, seek mutual benefits, question, understand.

SAMPLE BELIEFS AND LANGUAGE

- I don't win unless everyone wins; therefore, "Let's continue to explore until we all are satisfied with the solution."

- There is always a way to satisfy all the partners; therefore, "We can figure out how to do this so that each of us feels right about our approach."

- Conflict can be a good thing for discovering new ideas; therefore, "I'm glad you're sticking to your guns. We will ultimately come up with a better outcome."

- It is my responsibility to get my needs met; therefore, "I'm not ready to drop this and I want to explore further how we might approach this."

IMPACT

A partnership that supports win-win outcomes will maximize the quality of its output and the creativity of its members. When everyone feels that his or her needs are met, energy is high and collaboration is at its best.

OUTCOME

Win-win.

STATEMENTS THAT CHARACTERIZE THE NEGOTIATOR STYLE (SEE PAGES 59–60)

4. I cooperate with others to help them achieve their goals.

10. When fixing a problem, it's important that people get what they want.

12. I try to reach consensus on issues between people.

21. When solving a problem, I am not satisfied until everyone involved agrees with the solution.

27. I talk about problems and ask for others' thoughts.

28. I feel best when everyone wins.

33. I am concerned about what others need.

40. I think it is important to discuss the issues and identify needs with everyone before solving the problem.

EXAMINING YOUR SCORE

Action Step Referring to the Win-Win Orientation Assessment Grid on page 62, indicate your scoring range for the Negotiator style and answer the questions below.

High _____   Medium _____   Low _____

If you scored in the low or Medium range, think of a recent situation that is not yet resolved.

Who are the people involved?

_____

What are their needs?

_____

What are your needs?

_____

How might you approach this situation to achieve a win-win outcome?

_____

Applying Assessment Results to Your Partnership

In order for you and your partner to reach win-win outcomes, you must share information about your current styles and plan how you will work toward win-win outcomes in the future.

Action Step To help you gain an understanding of your current styles and your partner's current styles and how to achieve more win-win outcomes in the future, complete the exercise below and reflect on any implications for future working agreements.

PROBLEM-SOLVING STYLE REVIEW	
1. Your most frequently used styles for problem solving and conflict resolution are:	
2. Your partner's most frequently used styles for problem solving and conflict resolution are:	
3. If both partners do not use a win-win approach, what can you do to move toward a Negotiator style?	
4. What can your partner do to move toward a Negotiator style?	
5. How will you know when you are moving away from a Win-Win Orientation?	
6. When are you most likely to move away from a Win-Win Orientation?	

7. When is your partner most likely to move away from a Win-Win Orientation?	
8. How will you communicate to each other that you are moving away from a Win-Win Orientation?	
9. How will you hold each other accountable for using a Win-Win Orientation in future problem solving?	
10. Do you need to renegotiate any past agreements that did not achieve a win-win outcome?	

4

Ability to Trust

We learn how to interact with one another from the moment we are born. Based on our earliest experiences, we recognize patterns of actions and reactions among our families, friends, and eventually our communities. Our safety and well-being depend on our ability to correctly interpret and respond to a complex system of symbols and signals. As we grow, we discover that we feel safe with some people and unsafe with others. We learn what kinds of reactions we can provoke. This system of predictable, reliable reactions is what binds the social order together and forms the foundation of trust.

When we violate established rules and expectations, or when we act arbitrarily or differently from our usual patterns, others become confused and sometimes upset. Depending upon the history and specific circumstances, such behavior can be experienced as a violation of trust.

In business, establishing trust can be difficult. A competitive culture often rewards businesses that act in new and unpredictable ways. Building successful partnerships requires maintaining a climate in which the parties know the limits of reliability and are sure that those limits will be honored.

Assessing Trust Orientation

Before beginning the assessment, it is important to distinguish between our Ability to Trust and our trust orientation. The former is a function of the dynamics of the partnership, while trust orientation refers to how each individual partner approaches the partnership.

The following series of questions is designed to help you understand how you approach new partnerships in terms of trusting others. This is information you will want to share with your partner early in the relationship to ensure that trust can be established and maintained. Proceed by completing the assessment on the following pages.

TRUST ORIENTATION ASSESSMENT

Directions

- Read the following statements and select the response to the situation that is most true for you.

- Select your response assuming the situation involves someone you have just recently met and do not know well.

- Think back on similar situations you've experienced to determine the most accurate response.

1. Someone tells me that they are highly skilled at something.

a. I believe them.

b. I take a "wait and see" attitude.

c. I think they are probably exaggerating.

2. Someone in my field asks to see the work I am currently doing.

a. I am not inclined to share that information.

b. I suggest that we meet to share samples of our work. Based on how that meeting goes, I will decide whether to keep my work or leave it with them.

c. I send them samples of my best work.

3. Someone is quite flattering about my work.

a. I am not sure whether or not they mean it.

b. I assume they are sincere.

c. I think they want something from me.

4. There was a time in my career when I went through a significant crisis period that left me with self-doubts for a while.

a. I do not tell most people about it.

b. I tell people about it if I am sure that they will not use it against me.

c. I usually don't hesitate to tell people about it.

5. A new colleague offers to draft a letter in both of our names.

a. Once we have agreed on the content, I ask that a copy be sent to me.

b. I want to see what goes out before it is sent.

c. I ask to see the letter before it goes out until I am more familiar with his style.

6. I am working on a project with a colleague and am required to do some things that I have not done before.

a. I do not tell my colleague and try to learn on my own.

b. I tell my colleague and ask her to teach me.

c. I tell my colleague only if I am certain she will not think less of me.

7. When it comes to my personal finances:

a. I will tell someone about them only when I know and trust him.

b. I never discuss them with others.

c. I talk about them freely, if appropriate.

8. If someone asks me a personal question that I am a little sensitive about:

a. I avoid the question.

b. I answer the question.

c. I answer the question, giving some but not all of the information.

9. If I am seeking advice about a major purchase:

a. I will listen to someone I don't know well.

b. I will listen to someone if I am sure they know what they're talking about.

c. I will research on my own.

10. I think that in general:

a. Most people are out only for themselves.

b. Most people have good intentions.

c. Some people are out only for themselves and some people have good intentions.

Assessment Score Sheet

Tally your numerical score for each item and enter it in the right-hand column in the space provided. Then add up your scores and enter the total score at the bottom.

1. a = 3 points	b = 2 points	c = 1 point	Points on #1 _____
2. a = 1 point	b = 2 points	c = 3 points	Points on #2 _____
3. a = 2 points	b = 3 points	c = 1 point	Points on #3 _____
4. a = 1 point	b = 2 points	c = 3 points	Points on #4 _____
5. a = 3 points	b = 1 point	c = 2 points	Points on #5 _____
6. a = 1 point	b = 3 points	c = 2 points	Points on #6 _____
7. a = 2 points	b = 1 point	c = 3 points	Points on #7 _____
8. a = 1 point	b = 3 points	c = 2 points	Points on #8 _____
9. a = 3 points	b = 2 points	c = 1 point	Points on #9 _____
10. a = 1 point	b = 3 points	c = 2 points	Points on #10 _____

Total Score _____

Interpreting Your Assessment Score

Trust orientation resides within the individual. Each of us has a predisposition about how we come to trust others, and some of us have difficulty ever really trusting more than a few people. Our trust orientation stems from experiences since our infancy. It's very difficult to change because we tend to hold fast to our mental maps. Only under extraordinary circumstances do we alter our orientation and attitudes about trusting others.

Action Step Compare the total score you entered on your score sheet with the scoring ranges below. Then proceed with the interpretive information that follows.

Understanding Your Total Score

25–30 Points: High trust orientation

16–24 Points: Moderate trust orientation

10–15 Points: Low trust orientation

None of these orientations to trust are right or wrong. They simply represent different approaches to building trust, and each has implications for the formation of partnerships.

If your trust orientation is high (25–30 points), you tend to initially trust others in relationships until you have a reason not to trust them, either from information you might have about them or because they do something to lose your trust. How much risk you are willing to take will vary according to the situation. For example, you may trust that someone will watch your luggage at the airport or give you correct change, but you may investigate the authenticity of someone who asks for a $5,000 contribution toward a charity you know nothing about.

If you scored in this range, you need to be cautious in two areas. First, do not trust beyond your willingness to take a risk. You must be aware that you will not always be right about someone and therefore do not want to trust them with information or property that could prove costly should you turn out to be mistaken.

Second, don't make assumptions and then get disappointed because the other person was operating under a different set of assumptions. When this happens, trust can be eroded. For example, you may trust a peer to prepare and deliver a presentation, so you provide only verbal input during the planning stages. Later, you find out that she did not provide samples of the product, which you consider to be a very important aspect of a good presentation. Or, you trust a neighbor to watch your daughter after school. You find out later that he allowed the child to watch a television program that she is not allowed to watch at home.

In both cases above, your peer or neighbor may in fact have behaved in an "unprofessional" or "irresponsible" manner. However, it might also be that their behavior was due to having a different set of assumptions. In such circumstances you will want to clarify your assumptions up front and make them more explicit the next time, rather than deciding that you no longer trust your peer or neighbor.

If your trust orientation is moderate (16–24 points), you tend to wait until you've had enough experience with others before deciding whether you trust or distrust them. People who score in this range feel that trust must be earned and are generally cautious until they have enough information to support a person's "trustworthiness." Their criteria for building trust vary. If you scored in this range and are forming a partnership, you will want to be clear on your own personal criteria for trust.

If your trust orientation is low (10–15 points), you tend to require a great deal of information over a long period of time before you can come to trust a person. People who score in this range feel that most people are untrustworthy and are skeptical about others' motives and intentions. They can also lack faith in their ability to discern who is trustworthy and who is not, in part because another person's motivations and intentions are not readily discernable. A person who thinks others are untrustworthy can continue to be "right" because it can never be proven otherwise.

For example, a peer offers to cover for you while you are on vacation. Your mental map tells you that he wants something from you. If sometime after you return he asks for your help with a problem, your mental map is reinforced even if the two events are totally unrelated.

Some people with a low trust orientation have a need to be meticulous in matters that affect them. These people tend to believe that if things aren't the way they want them to be, they only have themselves to blame. Therefore, they need to check and double-check any and all situations where they feel responsible.

When working with someone with a low trust orientation, others might feel like they are not trusted. In most cases, low trust is not about the individual perceived to be untrustworthy, but about the person with low trust. If you scored in this range, be sure to share this information with your partner so he or she does not take your behavior personally.

Action Step Now that you have interpreted your trust orientation score, answer the questions in the following exercise to gain additional insight about the impact of your trust orientation on partnerships, and share this information with your partner.

EXAMINING YOUR TRUST ORIENTATION

1. My trust orientation is: (circle one)	**Low**	**Medium**	**High**
2. My beliefs about giving trust are:			
3. My beliefs about people are:			
4. I trust people when:			
5. What my partner has to know about my trust orientation is:			

Ability to Trust As One of the Six Partnering Attributes

Ability to Trust is unique among the Six Partnering Attributes needed for a high PQ. It is the only attribute that resides in the partnership rather than in the individual. Ability to Trust results when partners consistently practice and use the other five partnering attributes: Self-Disclosure and Feedback, Win-Win Orientation, Future Orientation, Comfort with Change, and Comfort with Interdependence (see Figure 3).

FIGURE 3

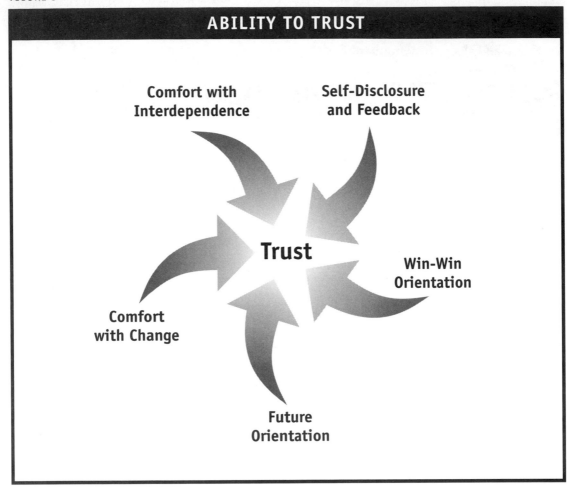

ABILITY TO TRUST

Comfort with Interdependence

Self-Disclosure and Feedback

Trust

Win-Win Orientation

Comfort with Change

Future Orientation

Assessing Ability to Trust

Because the Ability to Trust resides in the partnership, each partner contributes to the level of trust that is built in the partnership.

Action Step To gain a sense of the level of Ability to Trust that exists in a partnership, complete the assessment on the following pages. Keep in mind that this is not meant to be an evaluation. Rather, it is a tool by which partners can understand the dynamics of their relationship and continue to build trust.

ABILITY TO TRUST ASSESSMENT

- **The Ability to Trust Assessment is not a test with right or wrong answers.** It is descriptive rather than evaluative.

- **The Ability to Trust Assessment identifies specific behaviors that impact trust in partnerships.** It helps partners identify the criteria for trust in a specific partnership and act on them in order to enhance their trust. It is unlikely that any given partnership will demonstrate all the criteria for trust all of the time. It isn't necessary that there be the same level of trust in every partnership.

Directions

- Use the following scale to score each statement:

  1 = Strongly Disagree
  2 = Disagree
  3 = Somewhat Disagree
  4 = Somewhat Agree
  5 = Agree
  6 = Strongly Agree

- Enter your score in the column to the right of each statement *and* in the shaded box on the same line.

- Think about a specific partnership you're engaged in as you read the statements. Do not contemplate a statement too long. Your initial response is likely to be the most accurate one.

- Score the statements as honestly as you can. The extent to which this tool is useful depends upon how accurately it reflects what is actually true for you.

ABILITY TO TRUST ASSESSMENT

1 = Strongly Disagree   2 = Disagree   3 = Somewhat Disagree   4 = Somewhat Agree   5 = Agree   6 = Strongly Agree

Statement	Score	A	B	C	D	E
1. When my partner agrees to deliver something, he or she does it.			▨			
2. My partner listens to, and strives to understand, my point of view even if he or she disagrees with it.						▨
3. My partner believes this partnership is of value to him or her.		▨				
4. My partner is knowledgeable.					▨	
5. My partner tells me what he or she honestly thinks and feels.						▨
6. My partner works through problems and conflicts in order to maintain the partnership.		▨				
7. My partner gives me honest feedback, even if it's difficult.						▨
8. My partner keeps me fully informed of all information that pertains to the partnership.						▨
9. My partner does not say anything he or she does not mean.			▨			
10. My partner always delivers high-quality work.				▨		
11. My partner could not be enticed out of this partnership.		▨				
12. My partner meets deadlines.		▨				
13. I have confidence in the decisions my partner makes.				▨		
14. If my partner tells me something, I am confident it is true.					▨	
15. I always know when my partner thinks I've done a good job.						▨
16. I learn from my partner.		▨				
17. My partner is willing to invest time and energy to maintain the partnership.		▨				
18. My partner listens to, and considers, my feedback.						▨
19. My partner does not exaggerate to make himself or herself look good.					▨	
20. My partner appreciates how my success contributes to his or her success.			▨			
21. My partner is always on time.			▨			
22. My partner does not withhold or alter information in order to get his or her way.					▨	
23. My partner adheres to the terms of our agreements.			▨			
24. My partner accurately sizes up the events, politics, and interpersonal dynamics of most situations.				▨		
25. I can tell my partner things that are sensitive or might upset him or her.						▨
Total						

ABILITY TO TRUST ASSESSMENT (CONTINUED)

1 = Strongly Disagree   2 = Disagree   3 = Somewhat Disagree   4 = Somewhat Agree   5 = Agree   6 = Strongly Agree

Statement	Score	F	G	H	I	J
26. My partner does not judge or evaluate me.				▪		
27. My partner does not make unilateral decisions about matters that are in the joint interest of the partners.					▪	
28. My partner deals with emotional issues in a rational manner.					▪	
29. I know how my partner will react in conflict situations.		▪				
30. My partner accepts me as I am.					▪	
31. This partnership is as beneficial to me as it is to my partner.			▪			
32. My partner's behavior rarely surprises me.		▪				
33. My partner and I work well together.						▪
34. My partner readily acknowledges when he or she doesn't know something				▪		
35. My partner's efforts consistently add value.			▪			
36. I listen closely to my partner when we disagree because I am confident that he or she is motivated by the best interests of the partnership.					▪	
37. My partner brings as much to this partnership as I do.			▪			
38. My partner cares about meeting my needs and addressing my concerns.			▪			
39. I know my partner's strengths and weaknesses.		▪				
40. My partner values my opinions.					▪	
41. I can predict how my partner will act in a crisis.		▪				
42. My partner is always willing to go the extra mile to produce quality work.			▪			
43. My partner values and respects me as a person.				▪		
44. My partner does not exaggerate to make himself or herself look good.					▪	
45. My partner does not exaggerate in order to get his or her own way.						▪
46. My partner understands and accepts my shortcomings.				▪		
47. My partner readily admits when he or she makes a mistake.					▪	
48. I get as much from this partnership as I give it.			▪			
49. I'm able to influence my partner.					▪	
50. I can predict how my partner will think and feel about most things.		▪				
Total						

Assessment Score Sheet

The Ability to Trust Assessment provides an indicator of the overall level of trust in a relationship and also reflects the levels of trust in each of ten categories described on the following page that contribute to building successful partnerships.

Your Total Score

To obtain your total score, first add up the numbers in the first column ("Score") to the right of each statement and combine the totals here.

Page 86 Total _____

Page 87 Total _____

Total Score _____

Interpreting Your Assessment Score

Not every partnership requires the same level of Ability to Trust. The two variables that influence the necessary level of trust are the *importance* of the needs being met by the partnership and the extent to which that particular partnership is *required* to meet those needs.

Action Step Compare the total score you entered on your score sheet with the scoring ranges shown. Then proceed with the interpretive information that follows.

Understanding Your Total Score

130–150 Points: Very high Ability to Trust

109–129 Points: High Ability to Trust

92–108 Points: High–moderate Ability to Trust

67–91 Points: Moderate Ability to Trust

46–66 Points: Low Ability to Trust

25–45 Points: Very low Ability to Trust

The Ten Categories of Trust

If your partnership's current level of Ability to Trust is less than that required to meet your needs, you and your partner must enhance the Ability to Trust. Neither of you can do this alone. By definition it is a joint effort.

The Ten Categories of Trust that are measured in the Ability to Trust Assessment and discussed in detail in the following pages can help you and your partner determine what can be done by each of you to elevate the Ability to Trust in your partnership.

TEN CATEGORIES OF TRUST

Begin by determining your average score in each of the Ten Categories of Trust by completing the steps below. Remember that your score reflects your experience of your partner and vice versa.

To obtain your average score for each of the ten categories, add up the numbers in the shaded boxes in each column (A–E and F–J) on pages 86–87, then enter the totals here and divide by 5.

	Total	Average
Column A: Commitment to the Partnership	_____ /5 =	_____
Column B: Commitment to Keeping Agreements	_____ /5 =	_____
Column C: Competence	_____ /5 =	_____
Column D: Candor	_____ /5 =	_____
Column E: Communication	_____ /5 =	_____
Column F: Consistency	_____ /5 =	_____
Column G: Contribution	_____ /5 =	_____
Column H: Compassion	_____ /5 =	_____
Column I: Credibility	_____ /5 =	_____
Column J: Collaboration	_____ /5 =	_____

Now transfer your average scores to the Ten Categories of Trust Analysis Grid on the following page.

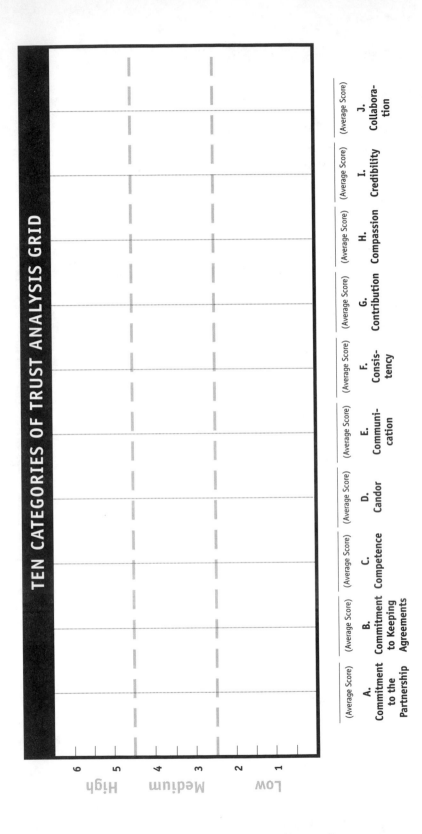

TEN CATEGORIES OF TRUST ANALYSIS GRID

High 6

5

Medium 4

3

2

Low 1

(Average Score)	(Average Score)	(Average Score)	(Average Score)	(Average Score)	(Average Score)	(Average Score)	(Average Score)	(Average Score)	(Average Score)
A. Commitment to the Partnership	B. Commitment to Keeping Agreements	C. Competence	D. Candor	E. Communi- cation	F. Consis- tency	G. Contribution	H. Compassion	I. Credibility	J. Collabora- tion

The Ten Categories of Trust Analysis Grid gives you a profile of your level of trust in each of the ten categories.

To Complete the Grid

Start with the first category, "Commitment to the Partnership," and note your average score on the vertical line above it. Continue until you have noted all ten categories on the appropriate vertical lines. Then connect the dots to get a profile of your Ability to Trust. The grid is divided vertically into three sections—low, medium, and high—to indicate the partnership's Ability to Trust in each category.

Your partner can also score his or her results on the same grid in another color to help you visualize how each of you is experiencing Ability to Trust in the partnership.

Understanding the Ten Categories Within Your Ability to Trust

COMMITMENT TO THE PARTNERSHIP

A high level of commitment to the partnership creates focus, creativity, and synergy among the partners. *Commitment* is measured by what each partner invests in the partnership in terms of time, energy, money, risk, and intellectual property.

COMMITMENT TO KEEPING AGREEMENTS

It is important that partners keep their agreements about what they will do and when and how they will do it. This allows each partner to focus on his or her own contribution with the confidence that the other partner will also deliver. If we do not keep our agreements, others might feel that they don't have to keep theirs. A relationship that does not honor agreements is ultimately undermined.

COMPETENCE

It is important that each partner believes that the other is competent both in his or her area of expertise and in general. Motivation is increased when each partner feels valuable and valued. If we get messages from others that they think we lack competence, we will put less and less energy and enthusiasm into the partnership. In addition, if we doubt the competence of our partners, we will eventually come to resent the feeling that they are unable to bring the necessary value to the partnership. Respect for the competence of each partner is therefore essential to a successful partnership.

CANDOR

A partnership is severely limited if each partner cannot feel that the other is telling the truth. Truth is not an absolute standard, but rather what is real for a person at any given time. A partnership thrives when partners can believe in what is true for each other.

COMMUNICATION

Communication is the process by which all partners have equal access to accurate and complete information relevant to the partnership, including "hard" and "soft" information. Hard information is tangible and refers to events, products, services, competition, and so on. Soft information is intangible and includes thoughts, feelings, intentions, values, and attitudes.

The larger the number of partners, the more important it is that the infrastructure support communication between all partners. Close attention must be paid to prevent situations in which some partners have more information than others. Even if such an occurrence is completely innocent, it can breed suspicion and distrust.

CONSISTENCY

Over time partners come to have expectations about the thoughts, actions, and reactions of the others in the partnership. It is important that each partner feels he or she can predict the behavior of the others. This predictability builds trust and facilitates communication, decision making, and productivity within the partnership.

Conversely, erratic behavior creates confusion and distrust and will undermine the effectiveness of the partnership. People cannot be as creative, efficient, or productive when they are unsure how their partners will behave.

CONTRIBUTION

In successful partnerships, people feel the value they add and the benefits they receive are equitable for all partners. Resentment and conflict result when that is not the case.

Contribution includes all the other categories that constitute Ability to Trust, and more. It can include hospitality, a sense of humor, graciousness, and any other positive traits one brings to a relationship. It is the sum total of how each partner adds value to the partnership.

COMPASSION

Compassion refers to the extent to which partners deal with one another as human beings. This means they accept and value each other's strengths and weaknesses without judgment and with sensitivity to personal consideration. In partnerships between neighbors, friends, and significant others, the purpose of the partnership is to treat each other with compassion.

The same is not true of partnerships that are formed to meet project or business needs. The focus of the partnership in these situations is on the output or outcome. Relationship issues are addressed in terms of how they impact that output or outcome. Such business partnerships do not require a high level of compassion, but they are much more effective if they include it. All of us appreciate being considered first as people. The comfort of being accepted as who we are will free energy and creativity that benefit the partnership.

CREDIBILITY

While *candor* refers to the accuracy of communication, *credibility* refers to the intent of the person offering it. Partners need to feel confident that information being offered to the partnership will contribute to the relationship as opposed to meeting the needs of the person offering it.

For example, if your partner says, "I think Jason lacks confidence in you," you may believe the information is candid. Your reaction, however, will depend on whether the statement was offered to make your partner look good or to enhance the output of the partnership. Lack of credibility undermines the dynamics of the partnership and thus the quality of what it can achieve.

COLLABORATION

Collaboration addresses the extent to which partners feel included in the dealings of the partnership and whether they have equitable influence in decision making. Partners need to feel that their opinions are listened to and respected. This is taken to be a measure of the value they bring to the partnership and also represents their ability to get their needs met.

When people do not feel that they can influence their partners, they feel powerless and resentful. This can lead to open and irresolvable conflict, or even sabotage on the part of the partner who feels "left out."

Consider a current partnership and complete the statements in the exercise below to suggest any needed changes to build trust in your partnership.

ENHANCING ABILITY TO TRUST

The level of Ability to Trust necessary in this partnership is:

_____

_____

The actual level of Ability to Trust is:

_____

_____

In examining the Ten Categories of Trust Analysis Grid, the categories that detract from Ability to Trust are:

_____

_____

For each category answer the following:

• What can my partner do to increase trust in this category?

_____

_____

• What can I do to increase trust in this category?

_____

_____

• How will we measure our progress?

_____

_____

• How will we define our success?

_____

_____

5

Future Orientation

We all learn from past experience—and indeed we should. This is called *knowledge transference* and it is essential to our effectiveness in the world. Without it, we would have to learn every situation, circumstance, and task anew every time we encountered it. We would never progress. Therein lies the value of knowledge transference.

A pitfall is the tendency to refer *only* to our past experience when we encounter a familiar situation, circumstance, or task. We all create mental maps—that is, expectations based on past experiences that determine how we approach similar experiences in the future. Often we are unaware of our mental maps, and it is not at all unusual to be emotionally invested in them. We have assigned them value and they represent what is "right" or "good" or "proper."

When we are unaware of, and/or attached to, our mental maps, two things almost always happen. The first is that we ignore or discredit any information that isn't consistent with our mental map. The second is that we therefore continually re-create the past. A Future Orientation frees us from this self-fulfilling prophecy and allows us to influence new and better outcomes.

Our orientation determines many aspects of a partnership before we even sit down to work with our partner. It determines how flexible we will be, how trusting, and how much risk we are willing to take. Smart partners know themselves well enough to keep from getting trapped in the past, and they trust themselves enough to make new plans and try different approaches. In order for us to get the most out of our partnerships, we must be aware of our reliance on Future Orientation and willing to open ourselves up to change and possibility. Otherwise, we risk finding out we're racing down the highway of life—and making decisions—based on what we see in the rearview mirror.

Assessing Future Orientation

Action Step To assist you in exploring your attitudes and beliefs regarding Future Orientation, complete the Future Orientation Assessment and proceed with the interpretive information that follows.

FUTURE ORIENTATION ASSESSMENT

- The Future Orientation Assessment is not a test, but rather a tool for exploring how you tend to act in relationships.

- For this tool to be useful to you, it is critical that you respond honestly—not as you think you "should."

Directions

Circle the response that you feel you would most likely make in the situations described in each of the items below.

1. I am working on a project and a fellow team member does not follow through on a promise. I will:

a. Not count on him and do what needs to be done myself.

b. Express that I expect him to keep his commitments.

c. Check in with him before a deadline to make sure he is doing what he's supposed to.

2. I am seeking a partner with project management skills and experience and need to choose between Judy, someone with outstanding skills who has sabotaged me and others in the past, or Frank, who has moderate skills but in whom I have more trust. I will:

a. Select Judy, explain the level of cooperation I need, and trust that I will get it.

b. Select Judy, explain the level of cooperation I need, and keep a close eye on her.

c. Select Frank.

3. I am asked by a colleague to participate on a task force to improve our company's performance management system. I tried the same project several years ago with little success. I will:

a. Tell him management is not likely to give more than lip service to the effort and he should forget the whole thing.

b. Agree to work on the task force but hold out very little hope of success so that I won't be disappointed again.

c. Agree to work on the task force and do my best, confident that we can gain management support.

4. My significant other is forgetful about entering checks written on our joint account. I get a notice from the bank that the last seven checks written on that account have been returned for insufficient funds. I will:

a. Call my partner at work to tell him or her to straighten this out.

b. Wait until my partner gets home in the evening to confront him or her.

c. Call the bank to find out what the problem is.

5. I am asked to participate on an exciting project that plays to my strengths but requires work in areas I do not enjoy and therefore am not strong in. I will:

a. Accept the assignment and develop a plan to improve the skills that I'm lacking.

b. Accept the assignment and get someone else to do the work in the areas where I am weak.

c. Turn down the assignment because "I'm just no good" at those skills.

6. I am working in partnership with Sam, who is a strong contributor but has poor computer skills. I will:

a. Offer to do his computer work because the value of his contributions is so high and no one can be good at everything.

b. Offer to teach Sam the necessary computer skills.

c. Add a third person who can do the computer work.

7. Every time I travel on business, everything goes wrong. I lose my luggage, have trouble with my hotel reservations, and often miss my plane connections. I will:

a. Plan more carefully and double-check ahead of time to make sure everything is taken care of.

b. Remind myself to keep my sense of humor and try to relax.

c. Refuse to travel on business unless it's absolutely necessary.

8. My neighbor breeds collies, and I decide to purchase one. After a year, the dog comes down with a rare and fatal form of cancer. I will:

a. Decide never to get another pet, because it's just too painful when they die.

b. Grieve the loss and make no decision one way or the other about getting another dog.

c. Sue my neighbor.

9. I have been asked to take the lead on a special project. I have done similar projects in the past, and they have all turned out to be extremely successful. I will:

a. Accept the responsibility, provide input, and look to the team members to plan and execute the project.

b. Accept the responsibility and plan the project as I have in the past, and look to the team members to execute it.

c. Refuse to do it, because it is "old hat" and would not be challenging.

10. A friend and I are cooking dinner together. We are preparing a main dish that has been in my family for generations. He suggests adding some new ingredients and cooking it on the grill rather than in the oven. I will:

a. Be eager to improve the recipe.

b. Listen politely, but be hesitant to try something new when my method is already delicious.

c. Explain that I learned this dish from my grandmother and it is a family tradition to prepare it this way.

Understanding the Future Orientation Assessment Statements

Each statement on the Future Orientation Assessment reflects a situation that forces a response to reveal something about your mental maps. Your responses are indicators of how much you may or may not rely on past experience to guide your behavior in a new situation and to what extent you are willing to open yourself to change, try new approaches, exercise flexibility, and trust in possibilities.

To better understand your own Future Orientation Assessment results, review the following statements and the analysis for each, noting any part of the interpretation that may be particularly meaningful to you.

1. I am working on a project and a fellow team member does not follow through on a promise.

In this situation, "Express that I expect him to keep his commitments" (b) indicates a Future Orientation. By focusing on the behavior you need, therefore expect, as opposed to the behavior you have experienced in the past, you are not permitting your partner to do anything other than follow through.

If you do his work for him (a) or continually check up on him (c), you are essentially communicating that you do not expect him to keep his word and are therefore taking responsibility to ensure that he does. This removes the accountability from your partner and places it on you, creating a situation that is self-perpetuating.

2. I am seeking a partner with project management skills and experience and need to choose between Judy, someone with outstanding skills who has sabotaged me and others in the past, or Frank, who has moderate skills but in whom I have more trust.

This situation is similar to the one above in that a Future Orientation requires that you focus on what you expect, rather than on what you have experienced before. If you select Judy, explain the level of cooperation you need, and trust that you will get it (a), you immediately set up the expectation that she will be a fully cooperative and contributing member of the team. Thus you create a situation where there is no permission for her to be otherwise.

If you select Judy and watch her closely (b), you are taking responsibility for her behavior. In addition, you will inevitably communicate your perception of her as untrustworthy. People usually behave according to our expectations of them, so your expectation actually influences her behavior. If you select Frank (c), you undermine the quality of the project without giving Judy an opportunity to change her behavior.

3. I am asked by a colleague to participate on a task force to improve our company's performance management system. I tried the same project several years ago with little success.

Working on the task force, doing your best, and expecting success (c) indicates a Future Orientation. If you work on the task force with little enthusiasm (b), your attitude will affect others' performance and ultimately the success of the project, reinforcing your original premise. If you resist undertaking the project at all (a), you are succumbing to your past experience and preventing any chance for things to be different in the future.

4. My significant other is forgetful about entering checks written on our joint account. I get a notice from the bank that the last seven checks written on that account have been returned for insufficient funds.

If you call the bank to check out the problem (c), you are not making assumptions based on past experience. It is possible that you forgot to make a deposit, or that there is some other explanation. If, after you talk to the bank, it does turn out that your partner has failed to enter checks, when you discuss it with him or her you are not communicating that you automatically assumed that overdrafts were the result of his or her mistake. If you call your partner at work (a) or confront him or her in the evening (b) prior to checking with the bank, you are inferring that you expect him or her to be at fault.

5. I am asked to participate on an exciting project that plays to my strengths but requires work in areas that I do not enjoy and therefore am not strong in.

Accepting the assignment and being accountable for improving certain skills (a) represents a Future Orientation. To turn it down (c) or get someone else to do the work in the areas that you are weak in (b) indicates the belief that you cannot progress or improve and that you will "always be that way."

6. I am working in partnership with Sam, who is a strong contributor but has poor computer skills.

If you offer to teach Sam to be more proficient on the computer (b), your focus is on the future. To add a third person to the project (c) or do Sam's work for him (a) communicates to Sam that, based on the past, you don't think he can acquire the necessary skills.

7. Every time I travel on business, everything goes wrong. I lose my luggage, have trouble with my hotel reservations, and often miss my plane connections.

If you assume that things will go wrong and think you need to rely on your sense of humor to get through it (b), or surrender and not travel on business (c), you are being driven by a past orientation. You can take a Future Orientation and assume that everything will go smoothly. To that end, you take control, plan carefully, and double-check everything before you go (a).

8. My neighbor breeds collies, and I decide to purchase one. After a year, the dog comes down with a rare and fatal form of cancer.

We all experience loss and disappointment in life. It's part of the package. However, if we let those sad experiences dictate our future choices, we cheat ourselves out of future joy. When we are in pain, if we simply accept it and let it pass (b), we are open to good times in the future. If we decide to guard against the pain (a), we are letting the past deprive us in the future. Or, if we decide to retaliate (c), we are simply prolonging the pain and holding onto the past instead of getting on with enjoying the future.

9. I have been asked to take the lead on a special project. I have done similar projects in the past, and they have all turned out to be extremely successful.

When we have done something quite successfully in the past, it is tempting to rely on what worked then (b). However, there are two risks to this. The first is that we simply re-create, rather than improve upon, what we've done previously. The second is that our partners become demotivated because they have little or no input. When we decide not to do something we have done before because it's "too easy" or we "could do it in our sleep" (c), we are not relying on a Future Orientation that says we can do it better. When we look to team members to plan the project as well as implement it (a), we bring something new and challenging to the task.

10. A friend and I are cooking dinner together. We are preparing a main dish that has been in my family for generations. He suggests adding some new ingredients and cooking it on the grill rather than in the oven.

When we have established what feels like a "tradition," we are especially tempted not to change it in any way. Often this is related to holidays and family rituals. We feel that if we do things differently, we will be losing something (b and c). Indeed, this might sometimes be the case. However, if we refuse to experiment, we are eliminating another possibility: discovering something new and perhaps better (a). Remember, we can always decide to go back to the old way.

The Influence of Language on Future Orientation

The language we use often indicates how we think and frequently guides our decisions and subsequent behavior. Attitudes and beliefs often change slowly and can be difficult to alter, but we can choose to change our behavior, no matter what our attitudes and beliefs might be.

Our language provides us with clues about the extent to which we use a Future Orientation in determining what actions to take. Language can be verbal, what we say, or nonverbal, what we think. Sometimes the influence of our language on our behavior is obvious. Other times, it is more subtle.

To help you understand how language might have influenced your responses on the Future Orientation Assessment, review your answers to each of the ten situations. The following pages offer examples of past orientation and Future Orientation thoughts or language that would influence behavior. Pay special attention to those situations where you would have responded from a past orientation.

PAST AND FUTURE ORIENTATION LANGUAGE

1. I am working on a project and a fellow team member does not follow through on a promise.

Past Orientation Language

"Next time, I'll know better than to count on him."

"I knew I should have done it myself!"

"I'll get someone else to do it next time."

Future Orientation Language

"He must not have known how important it was."

"Maybe he wasn't clear about the deadline."

"I'm sure he can come through moving forward."

2. I am seeking a partner with project management skills and experience and need to choose between Judy, someone with outstanding skills who has sabotaged me and others in the past, or Frank, who has moderate skills but in whom I have more trust.

Past Orientation Language

"I can't risk being undermined by Judy."

"She's always been sneaky and out for herself."

"I'd be a fool to count on her after what she's done to me before."

Future Orientation Language

"I want the best person for the job, and Judy is it."

"I think Judy can be trustworthy if given a chance."

"I think I might have misjudged Judy."

3. I am asked by a colleague to participate on a task force to improve our company's performance management system. I tried the same project several years ago with little success.

Past Orientation Language

"The management in this company never has been interested in employee input."

"I don't know what makes him think he can do a better job than I did."

"I just don't want to do all that work for nothing."

Future Orientation Language

"I can do a better job this time."

"The time is right to try this again!"

"I'll bet the others on the task force will have great ideas on how to make this happen."

4. My significant other is forgetful about entering checks written on our joint account. I get a notice from the bank that the last seven checks written on that account have been returned for insufficient funds.

Past Orientation Language

"I knew he'd do this again!"

"I'm going to take the checkbook away from her!"

"He'll just never learn."

Future Orientation Language

"Maybe this was my doing. I'd better check it out."

"I know she's been working on entering every check."

"He doesn't like this any better than I do."

5. I am asked to participate on an exciting project that plays to my strengths but requires work in areas that I do not enjoy and therefore am not strong in.

Past Orientation Language

"I never have been good at this."

"This just isn't my area."

"I'm good at other things, so I don't have to worry about this."

Future Orientation Language

"This is a perfect opportunity for me to get better at this."

"I know I don't like doing this, but it's something I need to learn."

"I can do this if I put my mind to it."

6. I am working in partnership with Sam, who is a strong contributor but has poor computer skills.

Past Orientation Language

"Sam just isn't good at this stuff."

"Some people just don't want to learn."

"I'm tired of people not living up to my standards."

Future Orientation Language

"I'm sure Sam could improve his computer skills."

"I know Sam wants to feel he is making a full contribution."

"Sam never was one to impose on others."

7. Every time I travel on business, everything goes wrong. I lose my luggage, have trouble with my hotel reservations, and often miss my plane connections.

Past Orientation Language

"I guess I just don't have good travel karma."

"I don't know why these things always happen to me."

"I'm better off when I don't have to travel!"

Future Orientation Language

"I'm going to plan carefully because I have control over my business travel."

"This time I will see to it that there are no mishaps."

"I can't wait to meet with that client. He's going to be very impressed with what we've done."

8. My neighbor breeds collies, and I decide to purchase one. After a year, the dog comes down with a rare and fatal form of cancer.

Past Orientation Language

"I never want to go through anything like this again. No more dogs for me."

"I guess I'm just not lucky when it comes to choosing pets."

"Next time I'll get a bird. I won't get as attached to a bird."

Future Orientation Language

"Life goes on."

"This is a tough time, and I will get through it."

"I know this too shall pass."

9. I have been asked to take the lead on a special project. I have done similar projects in the past, and they have all turned out to be extremely successful.

Past Orientation Language

"I might as well accept. I can do this in my sleep."

"I've done this too many times. There's no challenge to it."

"I can dig out my old files and have this thing put together in a heartbeat."

Future Orientation Language

"I'll do it again, and it will be bigger and better than ever before."

"With the input of others, what an opportunity to outdo myself!"

"I want to make sure I have people full of new ideas on the project."

10. A friend and I are cooking dinner together. We are preparing a main dish that has been in my family for generations. He suggests adding some new ingredients and cooking it on the grill rather than in the oven.

Past Orientation Language

"He's always insinuating he's a better cook than I am."

"I can see my entire ancestry turning over in their graves."

"Hasn't he ever heard 'If it ain't broke, don't fix it'?"

Future Orientation Language

"That's a good idea. We should try it."

"I'm ready to try something new."

"I guess good can always get better."

Past Orientation and Reliance on Mental Maps

Our tendency to rely upon a past orientation has helped human beings survive throughout our history. Our ancestors followed the herds and harvested the crops based on knowledge transference—using past experiences to help predict the outcome of future events. When we meet someone for the first time or have a new experience, we scan our memory for anything familiar about that person, place, or incident. We transfer knowledge from those experiences to help us decide our approach to the new person or situation. It's easy to understand how a past orientation has proven to be a powerful and successful strategy in adapting to life. However, in partnerships, one of the key objectives is to accomplish new and creative outcomes. In these cases, relying on past orientation can become a liability.

Mental Maps

Past orientation, like past experience, may be helpful in teaching us how to accomplish new tasks. Too often, however, people rely totally on past experience because they cannot give up the old and embrace the new. This behavior is due to a powerful human survival technique based on the use of mental maps.

Mental maps are more than simple, objective memories of past events. Our emotions, beliefs, values, and assumptions color them. Our mental maps influence our thoughts, which in turn influence our behaviors. Because our behaviors affect the outcome of events, we often create outcomes that reinforce our mental maps. Consider the following examples and the influence of mental maps in each situation.

Sara's Mental Map

Sara has an important sales presentation on Friday. She scans her memory for prior similar experiences. She has had many successful presentations prior to this in which she allowed adequate time to prepare, learned all she could about the potential client, and sought feedback from her peers. Sara believes she is bright and articulate, and she has received numerous comments about her excellent listening skills. Based on her mental map, Sara thinks: "I know I can win this account with adequate preparation and input from others. I am certainly good at presentations; I can listen for what the client is saying and can overcome both verbal and implied objections."

These thoughts spur Sara into action, and she begins to undertake the same thorough preparations she has used before. When she is up in front of the prospective client, she exudes confidence and professionalism. Because she is confident, she can focus on others in the room, concentrating on hearing and responding to what they need. Such behavior wins her the account and reinforces her mental map.

John's Mental Map

John is making his first sales presentation. He is fresh out of school, has just been hired to this position, and even though the company has provided new-hire training, he is quite nervous. While he has no mental map specifically related to sales, he scans his memory for prior events that have components similar to this one. He took a speech class in college and didn't like it at all. Every time he got in front of the class to speak, he would get nervous and flustered. He felt fortunate to have gotten a "C" in the class. His friends often joke that it takes him five minutes to communicate a one-minute thought. His parents expressed concern about him going into sales because he didn't have the "right stuff." John's mental map leads him to think: "I don't know why I ever got myself into this. I don't organize my thoughts well; I'm not good in front of people. What was I thinking?"

When John is preparing for the sales call, those thoughts keep running through his head and undermine his effectiveness in preparing the best possible presentation. During the call, he is nervous and self-conscious, actually making the prospective client uncomfortable. Of course, John does not get the sale. This experience supports his original mental map. Unless John can recognize his past orientation and make other choices, he is destined to fail in sales.

In Sara's case, it served her to rely on her past experience because it resulted in the outcome she wanted. John, however, could have made another choice. If he were aware of his mental map, he could have adopted a Future Orientation. In that case, he would have thought: "I have a lot of work to do to make this call a success. I must have the presentation ready well in advance so I have time to practice. I want to be able to do it in my sleep. I will also have to learn some relaxation techniques that I can apply immediately before the call. I think I'll invite my parents to dinner to celebrate my first sale!" With this attitude, John will perform more like Sara when he makes his presentation. He is planning to be successful.

In summary, our mental maps can have a powerful influence on behaviors as outlined in the steps below:

1. We are in a new situation.

2. We scan our memory for similar situations or ones that had similar components. We also scan for what we have been told about this new situation as well as our beliefs and assumptions. This is our mental map.

3. If we are in a totally new situation, we determine how to behave and begin the creation of a new mental map.

4. If the situation is similar to a past one, we categorize the past outcome as successful/desirable or unsuccessful/undesirable.

5. If we define that outcome as successful, we duplicate past behaviors, achieve desirable results, and reinforce our mental map.

6. If we define that outcome as unsuccessful, we determine the extent to which we feel the result was under our control.

7. If we conclude that it was the situation, not us, that determined the outcome, we will duplicate past behaviors that led to an unsuccessful outcome and reinforce our mental map.

8. However, if we conclude that we do have control in this situation, we can operate from a Future Orientation, increasing the probability of a successful outcome and the beginning of a new mental map.

The first step toward developing a Future Orientation, then, is to recognize our mental maps and the beliefs they represent, which enables us to change behavior. Very often the thoughts we harbor when faced with new situations provide powerful clues as to the mental maps and beliefs that are at work in the situation. Consider the following example:

New Situation

You walk into a department store and no one comes up to help you.

Thought

"Salespeople just don't care anymore. They are rude and indifferent to the needs of customers."

Beliefs

"Attention is a sign of good customer service."
"I need help from salespeople in order to find merchandise and decide what to purchase."

Mental Map

"In a retail store, salespeople should be immediately available to each customer and remain attentive to them throughout their shopping experience. When this does not happen, it means that the salespeople the outlet employs are rude and indifferent."

Behavior

Projecting obvious annoyance in your voice and body language, you approach a salesperson and demand proper service. Although the salesperson might comply, he or she will probably be offended by your comments and thus will provide a minimum of help, thus validating your mental map.

Alternative

You decide not to behave in accordance with your mental map. You approach a salesperson and politely ask for assistance. In this case, you are more likely to get courteous service and attention, which will thus challenge your mental map.

A Future Orientation is a critical factor in a successful partnership. Although our mental maps strongly determine how we approach situations and relationships, we can always choose to behave differently based on a future plan rather than past expectations. The more aware we are of our mental maps and how they influence our behavior, the more we are able to operate according to a Future Orientation.

ASSESSING YOUR MENTAL MAPS

1. What is your desired outcome, i.e., your future plan?

_____

_____

2. What are your thoughts about the situation, task, or partnership?

_____

_____

3. What past experiences have you had that are similar to the current one?

_____

_____

4. Was the outcome successful or unsuccessful?

_____

_____

5. If the outcome was successful, how do your thoughts (from #2 above) reflect this? Do you need to seek additional information or behavioral options to build upon past successes?

_____

_____

6. If the outcome was unsuccessful, how do your thoughts reflect this?

_____

_____

7. How can you change your behaviors, no matter what your thoughts, to effect a successful outcome?

_____

_____

6

Comfort with Change

In today's world, change is happening at an unprecedented rate. Accelerating social and technological advances have had a dramatic impact on us, and the ability to manage change is rapidly becoming a survival skill. By their very nature, partnerships inevitably involve change. This chapter will help you examine your attitude toward change and provide tools and exercises to help you to better manage it.

The Model for Managing Change

While change may be defined by the occurrence of a major event, it is in fact a dynamic process that occurs over time and consists of any number of smaller changes. As shown in Figure 4, managing change involves three phases, to be approached as follows.

- **Phase 1:** Begin at the end by identifying the future state

- **Phase 2:** Then, assess the current situation

- **Phase 3:** Finally, develop a transition plan to move from the current situation to the future state

Managing change begins with a vision of what an individual, department, or organization wants in order to achieve the future state. An assessment of the current situation identifies the gaps between the current reality and the vision of the future. The transition state is the time during which individuals or groups take action to move to the future state.

FIGURE 4

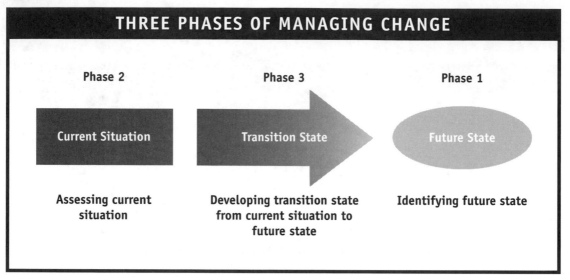

THREE PHASES OF MANAGING CHANGE

Phase 2	Phase 3	Phase 1
Current Situation	Transition State	Future State
Assessing current situation	Developing transition state from current situation to future state	Identifying future state

Partnerships are formed when they are necessary to achieve the vision of the future. They trigger many smaller changes during both the transition state and the future state. The changes may involve information flow and communication, systems and processes, individual roles and responsibilities, and formal and informal rewards.

Using the three-phase model for managing change just described, think of a change you would like to implement in your organization and complete the exercise below.

IMPLEMENTING CHANGE

1. Start with the future state (column 1) and think of what you want to achieve. Visualize the characteristics of the outcome and list them there.

2. Assess your current situation (column 2) and understand what you are currently capable of doing. Note your abilities and your limitations. It is important that your assessment is accurate in order to identify the gaps between your current situation and the desired future state.

3. List the tactics or actions required in the transition state (column 3) to achieve your future state. They will close the gap between what you have now and what you want to achieve.

| Current Situation | Transition State | Future State |

2	3	1
_____	_____	_____
_____	_____	_____
_____	_____	_____
_____	_____	_____
_____	_____	_____
_____	_____	_____
_____	_____	_____
_____	_____	_____

Assessing Change Orientation

Your mental maps about change largely determine your level of Comfort with Change. As described in the previous chapter, mental maps can lead to self-fulfilling prophecies. An understanding of your attitudes toward change is the first step toward increasing your ability to effectively manage it in partnerships.

> **Action Step** To get a sense of your own orientation to change, complete the following assessment.

CHANGE ORIENTATION ASSESSMENT

- **The Change Orientation Assessment is not a test with right or wrong answers.** It is a way to get an accurate portrayal of your orientation toward change. It is designed to be a tool to help you understand your attitudes and beliefs about change.

- **The Change Orientation Assessment is descriptive, not evaluative.** It describes your beliefs, attitudes, and orientation toward change. It is not meant to evaluate those beliefs, attitudes, or orientation.

Directions

- Circle the choice that describes you best.

- Do not contemplate a statement too long. Your initial response is likely to be the most accurate one.

- Rate the statements as honestly as you can. The extent to which this tool is useful depends on how accurately it reflects what is actually true for you.

1. When dividing the workload on a project, I prefer to:

a. Take on tasks that I've never done before.

b. Take on tasks that are familiar to me and do them in the way that has proved successful before.

c. Select tasks that are familiar to me and consider suggestions on how to approach them differently.

2. When I have leisure time, I prefer to:

a. Engage in activities I've done before and know I like.

b. Do things I've done before and occasionally try new things that friends have suggested.

c. Plan adventures that I've never done before.

3. When working with a partner or on a team, I am most comfortable when people:

a. Deviate from a plan only when the alternatives have been thoroughly explored and discussed.

b. Follow the plan.

c. Deviate from a plan as needed.

4. When dining out, I:

a. Try new and unique places.

b. Generally go to restaurants I am familiar with and try different dishes.

c. Go to restaurants I know and order my favorite items.

5. When I am in a new situation, I generally:

a. Feel exhilarated.

b. Am slightly nervous, but glad for a new experience.

c. Feel anxious and want to remove myself as soon as possible.

6. When doing a task that is new to me, I:

a. Use techniques I've used in the past.

b. Try things I've never done before.

c. Check with others for ideas.

7. Once I have learned to do something well, I:

a. Get bored with it and want to move on to something else.

b. Want to do it even more.

c. Experiment with different approaches.

8. When it comes to my daily routine, I:

a. Get frustrated if I get interrupted.

b. Don't mind if I get interrupted.

c. Don't really have a daily routine.

9. When driving to a familiar place, I prefer to:

a. Take the same route every time.

b. Try different routes and see new things.

c. Take the same route unless there are poor road conditions or heavy traffic.

10. When someone suggests a new way to do a familiar task, I:

a. Listen but will probably do it the way I always have.

b. Try not to be rude, but I really don't want to hear it.

c. Try it to see how it works.

11. When it comes to trying something new, I am likely to:

a. Try it after several of my friends have.

b. Just do it.

c. Move on without trying it.

12. I usually approach the day with a plan, and then I:

a. Look for opportunities to change it.

b. Change it if I have to.

c. Stick with it; I do not like to change plans.

13. When I am in a new situation, I tend to:

a. Jump right in and participate.

b. Watch others for a while and then start to participate.

c. Not participate much at all.

14. My friends would say that I:

a. Will try new experiences if coaxed.

b. Just don't want to do anything new.

c. Am always trying new things.

15. If I had my way:

a. Things would stay pretty much the same unless I chose to change them.

b. There would be constant change so I would never get bored.

c. Change would occur at a manageable pace.

Assessment Score Sheet

Tally your numerical score for each item and enter it in the right-hand column in the space provided. Then add up your scores and enter the total score at the bottom.

1. a = 3 points   b = 1 point   c = 2 points   Points on #1 _____

2. a = 1 point   b = 2 points   c = 3 points   Points on #2 _____

3. a = 2 points   b = 1 point   c = 3 points   Points on #3 _____

4. a = 3 points   b = 2 points   c = 1 point   Points on #4 _____

5. a = 3 points   b = 2 points   c = 1 point   Points on #5 _____

6. a = 1 point   b = 3 points   c = 2 points   Points on #6 _____

7. a = 3 points   b = 1 point   c = 2 points   Points on #7 _____

8. a = 1 point   b = 2 points   c = 3 points   Points on #8 _____

9. a = 1 point   b = 3 points   c = 2 points   Points on #9 _____

10. a = 2 points   b = 1 point   c = 3 points   Points on #10 _____

11. a = 2 points   b = 3 points   c = 1 point   Points on #11 _____

12. a = 3 points   b = 2 points   c = 1 point   Points on #12 _____

13. a = 3 points   b = 2 points   c = 1 point   Points on #13 _____

14. a = 2 points   b = 1 point   c = 3 points   Points on #14 _____

15. a = 1 point   b = 3 points   c = 2 points   Points on #15 _____

Total Score _____

Interpreting Your Assessment Score

Action Step Look at the total score you entered on your score sheet to determine which of the three orientations to change is most likely to resemble your own based on the ranges below. Then review the descriptors that follow to gain additional insight on the impact of each.

Understanding Your Total Score

38–45 Points: Initiator of change

23–37 Points: Adjuster to change

15–22 Points: Resister of change

Initiators

Initiators are people who not only have a high level of Comfort with Change, but also see change as an opportunity. They will often do things differently or do different things solely because of their need for change. In most cases, Initiators create and/or welcome change and do their best to make it work.

Sample Beliefs and Language

- Things usually happen for the best; therefore, "I think it's great that Mary was appointed to chair the committee."

- Life is exciting when it's unpredictable; therefore, "Let's not worry if we don't have our vacation plan all mapped out."

- I want to fully experience all life has to offer; therefore, "I always want to try new things and go different places."

If you are an Initiator, you find change exciting and will encourage it. You have no trouble accomplishing new tasks and working with new people under new and different sets of circumstances. Initiators must be careful that they don't impose change for its own sake. This can create unnecessary resistance from their partners and undermine the effectiveness of the partnership.

Adjusters

Adjusters adopt a "wait and see" attitude about change. While they don't enthusiastically embrace it, they are open to change if they see the value of it or if given some time. Adjusters want to be sure the change is permanent and necessary. They are more cautious than Initiators and tend to move more slowly when implementing change.

Sample Beliefs and Language

- I function best when things are predictable; therefore, "I'm not sure this change was really necessary."

- It is best to be cautious; therefore, "I don't understand why we're doing things this way."

- I want to be excellent at everything I do; therefore, "I prefer doing things the way I've always done them, because I know it works."

If you are an Adjuster, you will initially resist change or be hesitant to implement change, but as you learn more and become reassured over time, you will eventually support the change. Since change can represent risk, most people are Adjusters and vary only in the length of time it takes them to accept and support a specific change. According to how long it takes a person to implement change, he or she can be described as an early, middle, or late Adjuster. Adjusters must be careful not to sabotage the success of change before they give themselves the opportunity to accept and endorse it.

Rejecters

Rejecters refuse to acknowledge any need for, or value in, change. They behave as though a change has not occurred or is a mistake that needs to be corrected. Often, Rejecters campaign to engage others in their point of view with the intent to "get things back to how they were."

Sample Beliefs and Language

- Old dogs can't learn new tricks; therefore, "I see no point in trying to find new ways to do things."

- I must be in control; therefore, "I see no reason to try new approaches when the old way works just fine."

- There is a fixed set of rules, and I must follow these rules to be okay; therefore, "Let's do it the way we always have."

If you are a Rejecter, you are extremely uncomfortable with change and might deny not only the need for change, but that the change itself has actually occurred. You may tend to behave the way you always have because you are unable to accept the change. Rejecters must be careful that they do not diminish the value of their contributions because they refuse to embrace change. Once a significant number of people (a critical mass) supports the change, change will occur, and the Rejecters will be left behind.

YOUR CHANGE ORIENTATION

My change orientation style (Initiator, Adjuster, or Resister) is: _____

Think of a significant change in a partnership that resulted in a successful outcome.

• What was the change?

_____

• What needs did you want to fulfill through the partnership?

_____

• How did you feel at the beginning of the change?

_____

• What actions did you take to make the change successful?

_____

• How might your change orientation style have influenced your behavior?

_____

• How did you feel after going through the change?

_____

• What did you learn about yourself in regard to change?

_____

• How can you apply these learnings to future partnerships?

_____

Assessing Resistance to Change

While all individuals have their own unique mental map that explains their resistance to change, common themes or patterns often emerge. Change can represent risk, in that we have mental maps for staying "safe" and getting needs met.

Action Step A better understanding of our own resistance to change will not necessarily eliminate the anxiety that stems from change, but it can make our response to it more manageable. Complete the Change Resistance Assessment on the following pages to help you pinpoint the values that influence your Comfort with Change.

CHANGE RESISTANCE ASSESSMENT

- **The Change Resistance Assessment is not a test with right or wrong answers.** It is a way to get an accurate portrayal of what might influence your Comfort with Change in any given partnership.

- **The Change Resistance Assessment is descriptive, not evaluative.** We all have needs that are important to us. Society and our experiences growing up influence our needs; consequently, there is no such thing as a "good" or "bad" need. The Change Resistance Assessment is designed to help you understand your needs so you can better deal with the anxiety that arises in response to change.

Directions

- Use the following scale to score each statement:

  1 = Strongly Disagree
  2 = Disagree
  3 = Somewhat Disagree
  4 = Somewhat Agree
  5 = Agree
  6 = Strongly Agree

- Enter your score in the shaded box to the right of each statement.

- Do not contemplate a statement too long. Your initial response is likely to be the most accurate one.

1 = Strongly Disagree   2 = Disagree   3 = Somewhat Disagree   4 = Somewhat Agree   5 = Agree   6 = Strongly Agree

Statement	A	B	C	D	E	F
1. I would rather not do something if I cannot do it well.					▩	
2. I think money is a measure of a person's success.						▩
3. I get anxious when I drive in a city that is new to me.			▩			
4. If I feel responsible for the finished product, I like things done my way.		▩				
5. I work hard so others will think I'm successful.						▩
6. I still have friends from my youth.	▩					
7. I would rather do something I'm good at but am tired of, rather than do something new.					▩	
8. I will stay at a job I don't like rather than risk going without one.				▩		
9. I would leave a company before I would accept a demotion.						▩
10. I will do whatever it takes to keep from losing a relationship.	▩					
11. I will make substantial sacrifices now to make sure that my future is secure.				▩		
12. I like to make careful plans and have everyone follow them closely.		▩				
13. I like to do things well all the time.					▩	
14. I think people with a lot of power have done well in their lives.						▩
15. I am most comfortable when I know what to expect.			▩			
16. I like it best when things are done my way.		▩				
17. I am uncomfortable learning something new that I'm not good at doing.					▩	
18. I will tolerate behavior I don't like if I think that by saying something I risk losing the relationship.	▩					
Subtotal						

CHANGE RESISTANCE ASSESSMENT (CONTINUED)

1 = Strongly Disagree   2 = Disagree   3 = Somewhat Disagree   4 = Somewhat Agree   5 = Agree   6 = Strongly Agree

Statement	A	B	C	D	E	F
19. When something needs to be done right I am most comfortable if I do it myself.		▩				
20. I am a firm believer in "saving for a rainy day."				▩		
21. When I go to a restaurant I prefer to order something that I know I like rather than try something new.			▩			
22. If I could find a stable company, I would stay no matter what.				▩		
23. I will go to great lengths to avoid making a mistake.					▩	
24. I like it best when things are predictable.			▩			
25. I tend to save money rather than spend it, even if it's on something I can afford.				▩		
26. I will spend whatever time is required to stay in touch with people that I no longer see on a regular basis.	▩					
27. I will delegate tasks as long as they are done the way I think they should be done.		▩				
28. I think a person's title is an indication of his or her success.						▩
29. It is better to stay in a job I dislike rather than risk taking a new one that I might not like either.			▩			
30. There is absolutely nothing that would tempt me to move to a city where I did not know anyone.	▩					
Subtotal						
Page 126 Subtotal						
Total Score						

CHANGE RESISTANCE ASSESSMENT (CONTINUED)

Assessment Score Sheet

Subtotal your scores at the bottom of each column by adding up the numbers in the shaded boxes. Combine the subtotals, enter the total scores here, and divide by 5.

	Total	Average
Column A: Lasting Relationships	_____ /5 =	_____
Column B: Control	_____ /5 =	_____
Column C: The Familiar	_____ /5 =	_____
Column D: Future Security	_____ /5 =	_____
Column E: Mastery	_____ /5 =	_____
Column F: Status	_____ /5 =	_____

Now plot your average scores on the grid below to obtain your profile.

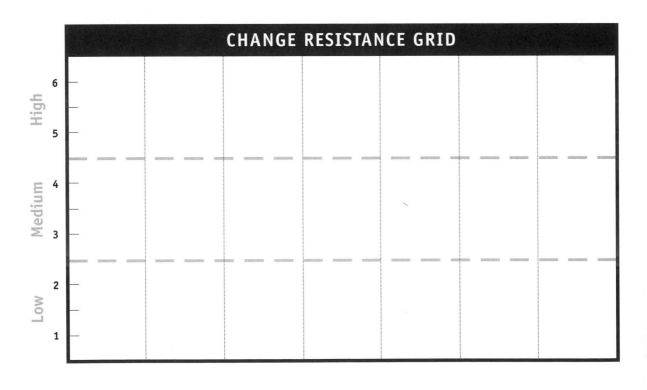

CHANGE RESISTANCE GRID

High — 6, 5
Medium — 4, 3
Low — 2, 1

_____ (Average Score)   _____ (Average Score)   _____ (Average Score)   _____ (Average Score)   _____ (Average Score)   _____ (Average Score)

A. Lasting Relationships   **B.** Control   **C.** The Familiar   **D.** Future Security   **E.** Mastery   **F.** Status

Interpreting Your Assessment Score

Very often we resist change because we are afraid that we will lose something important to us and that critical needs will be left unsatisfied. The Change Resistance Assessment measures six needs: lasting relationships, control, the familiar, future security, mastery, and status. The higher you scored on a need, the more likely you are to feel anxious when a change threatens it.

Lasting Relationships

People who value lasting relationships have a strong sense of personal history and put a lot of effort into keeping in touch, and getting along, with others who are part of that history. They feel a sense of continuity when interacting with people they have known for a long time through many stages of their life.

If you scored high on this need, you must be careful that you don't neglect new relationships in favor of older ones or that you don't pass up potentially advantageous partnerships for fear they will interfere with your long-lasting relationships.

Control

People who put a high value on control can find partnerships very challenging. By definition, partnering requires relinquishing some amount of control to achieve the full potential of the partnership.

If you scored high on this need, you must be careful that you don't demotivate your partner or neglect your own responsibilities in order to control the activities of others.

The Familiar

People who value the familiar are challenged when a partnership requires them to venture into the unknown. They are hesitant to engage in new activities or do things differently and will resist when asked to do so.

If you scored high on this need, you must be careful not to limit the potential of the partnership by disregarding opportunities because they take you out of your comfort zone.

Future Security

People who value future security are frugal and cautious about their finances. They are averse to taking any risks in this area and anxious in situations that they feel may threaten them financially.

If you scored high on this need, you will want to be circumspect about entering a partnership that puts you at financial risk. You will need to plan carefully how you will manage your anxiety if you do decide to get into such a situation.

Mastery

People who value mastery want to excel at what they do. In partnerships they want to feel like a valued contributor. When confronted with new tasks or skills, they will either reject them or work arduously to become good at them.

If you scored high on this need, you must be careful not to shy away from new ideas and activities because you have not yet mastered them.

Status

People who value status measure worth by money, title, and power and they want others to be aware of their accomplishments. Our society reinforces this perception; all of us, in some way, define success in terms of status.

If you scored high on this need, in partnership situations you might be inclined to focus more on status issues than on what is best for the results of the partnership.

Overcoming Challenges Related to Change

Let's examine two approaches to overcoming challenges from the changes that result from partnerships. The first approach involves managing these changes through individual strategies. The second involves managing them through partnership strategies.

Individual Strategies for Overcoming Challenges

The following exercises are designed to show what you can do on your own to manage the change required in partnerships. They essentially involve an awareness of your needs and the ability to be creative in how they are satisfied. Your specific needs may not be addressed here, but the same process can be applied by asking, "What do I require and how can I get it?" If it is not available in the partnership, get it elsewhere.

 **To gain a greater sense of control and mastery, complete the following exercises using the completed sample following as a model.**

FINISH WHAT YOU STARTED

Directions

- Make a list of tasks in your personal or professional life that you meant to accomplish but have not yet completed. These can be home-related, e.g., clean the garage; interpersonal, e.g., get feedback from your boss regarding a project; or intrapersonal, e.g., exercise regularly.

- Either complete these tasks or decide to delegate them to someone else, defer them to a later time, or not do them at all.

SAMPLE TASK AND STATUS LIST

TASK	STATUS
Complete expense reports	By mid-month
Prepare presentation for annual sales meeting	By end of week
Develop next quarter's budget	Delegate to Jack
Reorganize files	Not worth it!
Clean desk	Defer to beginning of year

TASK AND STATUS LIST

TASK	STATUS

Action Step If you are in a partnership where you feel your future security is at risk, it is important to manage your anxiety. Taking careful stock of your financial situation and doing some contingency planning can help you achieve a greater sense of control. Once you are clear on your financial situation, take one or all of the steps outlined in the exercise below.

REVIEW YOUR FINANCES

- Make a budget and carefully stick to it.

- If you are already on a budget, look for areas where you might cut back.

- Review your investments to ensure you are achieving maximum growth.

- If this partnership requires some amount of financial investment, decide how much you can afford to lose and do not go beyond that amount.

Action Step Complete the following exercise to reduce anxiety about loss or change in relationships and about the unfamiliar.

REWARD YOURSELF

- Make a list of people you like being with and recreational and/or restful activities you enjoy such as having coffee with a friend or going for a walk.

- Decide whether items on the list are "affordable," in that you have both the time and money to see these people or do these things.

- Make sure that you make time each day for these relationships and activities.

Complete this exercise to help ease anxiety in general and help with your need for mastery.

PUMP YOURSELF UP

- List your answers to the following two questions: "What do I most admire about myself?" and "What do others compliment me about?"

- The answers can include traits, skills, abilities, talents, or knowledge; e.g., sense of humor, conflict resolution, playing the guitar, knowledge of history, project management.

- Think of as many items as you can for both questions. It's okay to have overlaps.

- Once your list is complete, arrange to do those things or exhibit those traits. For example, if you admire your sense of humor, arrange a dinner party so you can exhibit it. Or, if you are complimented for your knowledge of history, start a club to read and discuss historical novels.

Partnership Strategies for Overcoming Challenges

In addition to your individual efforts to overcome challenges, you can contract with your partner about how you will deal with your challenges within the partnership.

Action Step **Think of a challenge in a current partnership, enlisting the help of a partner to complete the following exercise.**

THE PARTNERSHIP CONTRACT

My challenges related to change are:

_____

_____

My partner's challenges related to change are:

_____

_____

My specific concerns related to this partnership are:

_____

_____

My partner's concerns related to this partnership are:

_____

_____

What I need from my partner is:

_____

_____

What I will do for my partner is:

_____

_____

7

Comfort with Interdependence

The essence of interdependence is that what benefits the group benefits the individual, and vice versa. Each person in an interdependent relationship actively supports the success of another. Interdependent relationships are entered into when the parties involved need one another to meet individual needs and reach common goals. By definition, interdependent relationships require that people rely on one another.

Based on our beliefs and mental maps, we all have different levels of Comfort with Interdependence. Western society teaches us to value independence: "He got where he is today all by himself with no help from anyone else." In school we were often told to "do your own work." All of us take pride in our individual achievements and in being able to do things for ourselves. However, in partnerships, the greater the Comfort with Interdependence that exists among the parties, the greater the potential of the partnership.

Assessing Comfort with Interdependence

Action Step — Complete the following assessment to help you explore how comfortable you are with interdependence.

COMFORT WITH INTERDEPENDENCE ASSESSMENT

- **The Comfort with Interdependence Assessment is not a test with right or wrong answers.** It is a way to get an accurate portrayal of your tendencies when it comes to relying on others and having them rely on you. It is designed to help you understand your attitudes and beliefs about interdependence.

- **The Comfort with Interdependence Assessment is descriptive, not evaluative.** It describes your beliefs, attitudes, and orientation toward interdependence. This tool is not meant to evaluate those beliefs, attitudes, or orientation, but rather to help you understand how you deal with interdependence in partnerships.

Directions

- Use the following scale to score each statement:

  1 = Strongly Disagree
  2 = Disagree
  3 = Somewhat Disagree
  4 = Somewhat Agree
  5 = Agree
  6 = Strongly Agree

- Enter your score in the column to the right of each statement.

- Do not contemplate a statement too long. Your initial response is likely to be the most accurate one.

COMFORT WITH INTERDEPENDENCE ASSESSMENT (CONTINUED)

1 = Strongly Disagree 2 = Disagree 3 = Somewhat Disagree 4 = Somewhat Agree 5 = Agree 6 = Strongly Agree

Statement	Score
1. I prefer to make my own travel reservations.	
2. I actively seek opportunities to work with others.	
3. I am most comfortable when I am doing a project by myself.	
4. I seek the help of others only to do work that I do not know how to do.	
5. I enjoy doing a project more when it involves working with others than when I do it by myself.	
6. On a team project, I am most comfortable when I can double-check the work of my teammates.	
7. When giving a gift to a mutual friend, I am not concerned if someone else picks it out and I don't see it until it's opened.	
8. It is okay with me if a teammate sends something out without checking with me first.	
9. When I work with others I am comfortable if they do things differently than I would.	
10. When someone tells me something that I did not know, I usually check up to make sure that it is accurate.	
11. I tend to be a perfectionist.	
12. I believe that the best results are achieved when I work with others.	
13. Once I delegate a task, I rarely check up to make sure it is getting done.	
14. When driving to an unfamiliar place, I would prefer checking a map to relying on directions from a passenger.	
15. When working on a team, I pay most attention to the quality of my own work and leave my teammates to do their work.	
16. I want to work with others only when I cannot do it all myself.	

1 = Strongly Disagree   2 = Disagree   3 = Somewhat Disagree   4 = Somewhat Agree   5 = Agree   6 = Strongly Agree

Statements	Score
17. When preparing food for a dinner party with others, I am only concerned with what I'm making and don't worry about the other people's dishes.	
18. I do not think that most other people are as competent as I am.	
19. I think that most other people are as quality-conscious as I am.	
20. I do not want to rely on others unless I know from past experience that they will follow through.	

Assessment Score Sheet

Subset A

For the following, enter the scores you assigned on pages 141–42:

Statement 2 _____	Statement 9 _____	Statement 17 _____
Statement 5 _____	Statement 12 _____	Statement 19 _____
Statement 7 _____	Statement 13 _____	**Subtotal A** _____
Statement 8 _____	Statement 15 _____	

Subset B

For the remaining items, convert your rating to the score indicated and enter it in the space provided.

If you rated the statement a **6,** your score is **1.**
If you rated the statement a **5,** your score is **2.**
If you rated the statement a **4,** your score is **3.**
If you rated the statement a **3,** your score is **4.**
If you rated the statement a **2,** your score is **5.**
If you rated the statement a **1,** your score is **6.**

Statement 1 _____	Statement 10 _____	Statement 18 _____
Statement 3 _____	Statement 11 _____	Statement 20 _____
Statement 4 _____	Statement 14 _____	**Subtotal B** _____
Statement 6 _____	Statement 16 _____	

Subtotal A _____
Subtotal B _____
Total Score _____

Interpreting Your Assessment Score

Action Step Compare the total score you entered on your score sheet with the scoring ranges below. Then proceed with the interpretive information that follows.

Understanding Your Total Score

96–20 Points: High Comfort with Interdependence

71–95 Points: High–moderate Comfort with Interdependence

45–70 Points: Low–moderate Comfort with Interdependence

20–44 Points: Low Comfort with Interdependence

If you scored high on this attribute (96–120 points), you are not only comfortable in situations requiring interdependence, you actually seek them out. This could be because you are extroverted and prefer doing things with others or because you believe that collaboration produces a higher-quality result.

If you scored high–moderate on this attribute (71–95 points), you are generally comfortable with interdependence with the exception of situations where: (1) the stakes are exceptionally high; (2) there is something important to be gained by doing something on your own; or (3) you have reason to doubt the competence or commitment of others.

If you scored low–moderate on this attribute (45–70 points), you most likely prefer to work on your own unless the stakes are not particularly high or unless others have the capacity or expertise to do what you cannot.

If you scored low on this attribute (20–44 points), you would in most cases prefer to do things on your own.

YOUR COMFORT WITH INTERDEPENDENCE

1. My Comfort with Interdependence level is: _____

2. I am in this partnership because:

_____

_____

3. Our mutual goal is:

_____

_____

4. What I need from my partner is:

_____

_____

5. What my partner needs from me is:

_____

_____

The Balance of Interdependence

Through different stages in life we tend to view ourselves as either dependent or independent. As young children we are totally dependent on our parents, striving for independence as we grow into adulthood. We tend to look at ourselves as either wholly dependent or independent, but in most cases we are neither (see Figure 5).

FIGURE 5

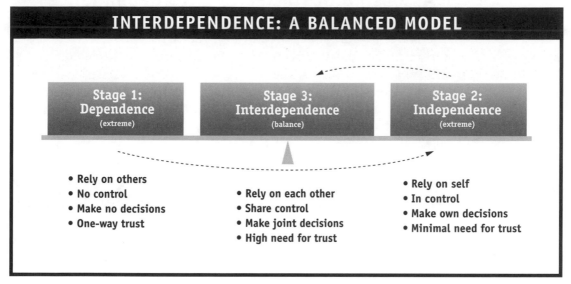

INTERDEPENDENCE: A BALANCED MODEL

Stage 1:
Dependence
(extreme)

Stage 3:
Interdependence
(balance)

Stage 2:
Independence
(extreme)

- Rely on others
- No control
- Make no decisions
- One-way trust

- Rely on each other
- Share control
- Make joint decisions
- High need for trust

- Rely on self
- In control
- Make own decisions
- Minimal need for trust

Dependence

When we are dependent, we feel we must rely on others for what we need. Therefore other people have control and make the decisions. This is a situation of one-way trust, where the dependent party has no choice but to trust the other party.

Independence

When we are independent, we rely totally on ourselves, have full control, and make all the decisions. There is no need to trust others.

Interdependence

There are very few life circumstances in which we are totally dependent or independent. Our society and the requirements for survival are much too complex for any of us to go it alone. Rather than being either dependent or independent, we can think of our interactions with others as being a balance of interdependence.

Interdependence can be supported by an agreement between parties, a contract between parties, or by an infrastructure. Interdependence by agreement or contract are informal or formal voluntary partnerships where the parties rely on each other to reach mutual goals. Interdependence by infrastructure most often refers to interdependence within a larger system, such as a government or organization.

Assessing Obstacles to Interdependence

People prefer to work independently for many reasons. Everyone has a unique mental map that explains his or her preference to work alone.

Action Step Complete the Obstacles to Interdependence Assessment to help you pinpoint some common needs that may influence your level of Comfort with Interdependence.

OBSTACLES TO INTERDEPENDENCE ASSESSMENT

- **The Obstacles to Interdependence Assessment is not a test with right or wrong answers.** It is a way to get an accurate portrayal of your tendencies when it comes to relying on others and having them rely on you. It is designed to help you understand your attitudes and beliefs about interdependence.

- **The Obstacles to Interdependence Assessment is descriptive, not evaluative.** It describes needs and beliefs that might interfere with your comfort in interdependent situations. It is not meant to evaluate those needs and beliefs. Rather, it is a tool to help you understand how they influence your behavior in partnerships.

Directions

- Use the following scale to score each statement:

  1 = Strongly Disagree
  2 = Disagree
  3 = Somewhat Disagree
  4 = Somewhat Agree
  5 = Agree
  6 = Strongly Agree

- Enter your score in the shaded box to the right of each statement.

- Do not contemplate a statement too long. Your initial response is likely to be the most accurate one.

1 = Strongly Disagree   2 = Disagree   3 = Somewhat Disagree   4 = Somewhat Agree   5 = Agree   6 = Strongly Agree

Statement	A	B	C	D	E	F
1. I take much more pride in my work when I do most of it myself, and if others make changes, they are minor ones.	▦					
2. I measure my abilities against those of others and I strive to be better than they are.					▦	
3. I don't like to do something unless I can do it exceptionally well.				▦		
4. I think less of a co-worker if he asks for help with something he's supposed to do by himself.	▦					
5. I don't like it when my teammates know more about something than I do.						▦
6. When working on a project, I want to know what each of my teammates is doing each day.			▦			
7. I strive to be better than others at what I do.					▦	
8. I don't like it if the team gets recognized for something that I did mostly by myself.				▦		
9. I keep going over my work until I am sure that I can't make it any better.			▦			
10. I would prefer to go without knowing how to do some things rather than reveal to others that I don't know how to do them.						▦
11. If my partner and I agree on how to do something and she decides to do it differently, I prefer that she check with me first.		▦				
12. If I complete a project by myself, I take more pride in it than if I have had help from others.	▦					
13. On a team project I want others to know specifically what my contributions were.				▦		
14. I strive to make my work as close to perfect as I can get it to be.			▦			
15. It is important to me that I win.					▦	
Subtotal						

1 = Strongly Disagree   2 = Disagree   3 = Somewhat Disagree   4 = Somewhat Agree   5 = Agree   6 = Strongly Agree

Statement	A	B	C	D	E	F
16. If a teammate is working on something and it is not as good as I think it should be, I prefer to make it over.		▨				
17. I get more satisfaction from projects I completed myself than from those I did with others.	▨					
18. It upsets me if someone takes credit for something I did.				▨		
19. If necessary, I will start something all over again in order to get it right.			▨			
20. When discussing the best way to go about accomplishing something, it is important to me to be "right."					▨	
21. It's hard for me to admit that I don't know something.						▨
22. It's important to me to have things under control.		▨				
23. Even if no one else would notice it, it bothers me if I know there is a minor flaw in something, and I will correct it.			▨			
24. I hesitate to ask a question if I think I "should" know the answer.						▨
25. I think more highly of someone else's work if they do it themselves.	▨					
26. I always strive to do better than others.					▨	
27. I like to be recognized for my work.				▨		
28. When working on a team project, I like daily progress reports from everyone involved.		▨				
29. When working on a task with someone else, I like it if I know more than they do.						▨
30. I would prefer to be recognized for my individual achievements more than to win an award for a team effort.				▨		
Subtotal						
Page 145 Subtotal						
Total Score						

OBSTACLES TO INTERDEPENDENCE ASSESSMENT (CONTINUED)

Assessment Score Sheet

Subtotal your scores at the bottom of each column by adding up the numbers in the shaded boxes. Combine the subtotals, enter the total scores here, and divide by 5.

	Total	Average
Column A: Individual Achievement	_____	/5 = _____
Column B: Control	_____	/5 = _____
Column C: Perfection	_____	/5 = _____
Column D: Individual Recognition	_____	/5 = _____
Column E: Competition	_____	/5 = _____
Column F: Expertise	_____	/5 = _____

Now plot your average scores on the grid below to obtain your profile.

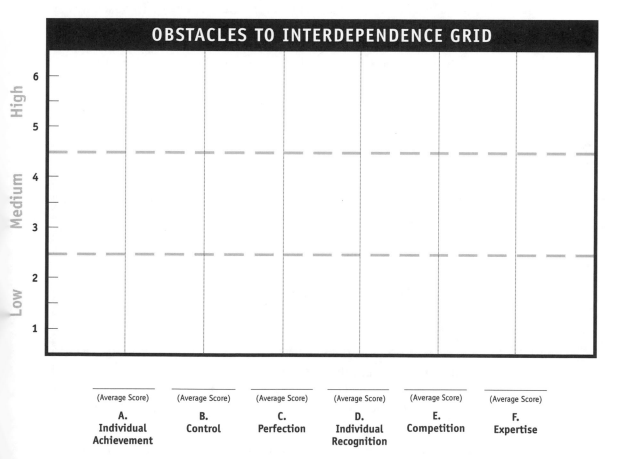

OBSTACLES TO INTERDEPENDENCE GRID

Interpreting Your Assessment Score

We often prefer to work independently because it allows us to achieve something important to us and to satisfy critical needs. The Obstacles to Interdependence Assessment measures six common needs: individual achievement, control, perfection, individual recognition, competition, and expertise. The higher you scored on a need, the more likely it will influence your behavior in partnerships.

Individual Achievement

People who value individual achievement will find partnership situations challenging when interdependence requires their individual efforts to become blurred with team contributions. If you scored high on this need, you believe that your efforts are somehow diminished if others have major input or share in doing the work. You prefer to work independently so that the end result reflects upon you and you can call it "your own."

People who value individual achievement often resist feedback if they feel it significantly alters their original concept. They are uncomfortable delegating or sharing responsibility for fear that doing so will change the way the finished product will look or that they won't be able to "own" the result. If you scored high on this need, you must be careful that you focus on the quality of the outcome and the need for others' contributions rather than on your own sense of individual achievement.

Control

If you scored high on this need, you are most comfortable when you feel you have control over what, how, and when things are done. As with Comfort with Change, people who value control have a difficult time with interdependence because it requires letting go of issues, approaches, and tasks that will impact the ultimate results of the partnership. If you place a high value on control, you will want to maintain your focus on your responsibilities and contributions to the partnership.

Perfection

Most of us take pride in the quality of our work. People who place a high value on perfection want things "right" to the smallest detail. They hesitate to call something finished unless they are sure it is close to perfect. In partnership situations they want others to adhere to the same high standards, and they might want to approve their partners' work. If you scored high on this need, you will want to be careful not to imply that you lack trust in, or respect for, the quality of your partners' work.

Individual Recognition

People who value individual recognition want to be acknowledged for any contributions they make toward a team effort. It is important for them to know that others appreciate their accomplishments. If you scored high on this need, you might prefer to do things independently so you can take full credit for the results. In partnerships, you will want to be careful that in your need for individual recognition you do not devalue the contributions of others.

Competition

People who value competition focus on outdoing others. They have a strong need to "win" and to compare themselves to others in order to do so. This can have a positive impact if the focus of the team or partnership is to win over the competition. If you scored high on this need, you must be careful not to foster competition within the partnership to the extent that it undermines the partnership's purpose and results.

Expertise

People who value expertise often feel that they "should" know a lot, especially in their own field. In partnerships they might feel uncomfortable if people are relying on them and they do not feel they know as much as their partners. Or, they may have problems relying on others that seem to know less than they do. If you scored high on this need, you must be careful not to denigrate your work or that of others based on superior knowledge or skills.

PART TWO

BUILDING SMART PARTNERSHIPS

Smart partnerships are built by design, not through evolution. Smart partners take a deliberate and purposeful approach to building partnerships. If you want a successful partnership, you need to be a smart partner.

Up to this point, we have focused on the individual, or the individual as a team member; you've worked to improve your Partnering Intelligence and learned how the Six Partnering Attributes accelerate your partnering success through the Stages of Relationship Development. Now it is time to put these relationship skills to work, using them to create the partnership that will help you accomplish your goals. In Part Two we focus on the partnering teams. We shift to the Stages of Partnership Development and the tasks you need to complete to build the foundation of a flourishing partnership.

The Partnership Continuum Model

We begin by reviewing the Partnership Continuum model. As shown in Figure 6, the model comprises two components. The Stages of Relationship Development—Form, Storm, Norm, and Perform—describe the processes

151

FIGURE 6

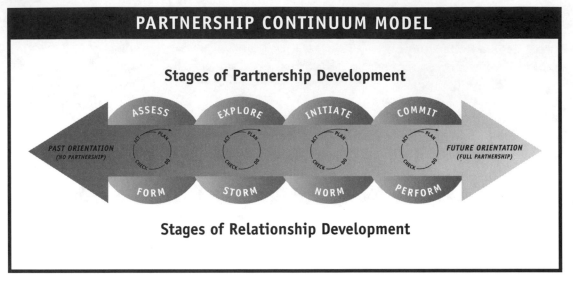

individuals need to go through to build trusting, mutually beneficial relationships. The Stages of Partnership Development—Assess, Explore, Initiate, and Commit—describe the tasks that partners must accomplish to create a successful partnership.

The model is to be read vertically as well as horizontally in order to assist the development of both tasks and processes, as shown in the diagram below.

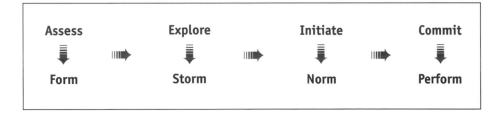

During the Assess Stage of Partnership Development, you are trying to understand your own organization's strengths and weaknesses. You are articulating a Strategic Framework and identifying your needs. It is critical during this stage that you and your team be honest and completely up-front with one another. If you don't bring up your weaknesses, count on your potential partners to do it for you. Avoid that at all costs—it will undermine the trust you've been able to establish so far.

You're also in the Form Stage of Relationship Development, when you are establishing your relationship. Using the JoHari Window (see p. 34) as a model for developing trust, your ability to honestly disclose your capabilities and give and receive feedback is a powerful tool for building trust between team members.

During the Explore stage you are approaching and qualifying potential partners. Being open to understanding their positions and building win-win outcomes here will be critical; but you must also trust that your partners are willing to help you achieve those outcomes.

While you are exploring, you are also entering the Storm Stage of Relationship Development. During the Storm stage is when conflicts erupt as people look for win-win solutions and assess their boundaries and needs. When your partners exert their needs, and solutions are harder to negotiate, you need to be skilled in moving to the Negotiator style (see p. 73) of problem solving and conflict resolution. To do this effectively, you must again trust that your partner is equally as interested in achieving a win-win outcome as you are, or you'll end up nowhere.

In the Initiate Stage of Partnership Development, you are implementing your project. This requires you and your teams to do new things and operate in new ways. Isn't that what the partnership is about?

Now, you're also in the Norm stage, when you begin to develop the norms of behavior and working agreements. While working on a task, you must be comfortable doing things in new ways and not reverting back to the old ways. Thus, the ability to have a Future Orientation and being comfortable with the change that creates will be critical to your relationship. Otherwise, you will begin the process of undermining the trust you've established.

In the Commit stage, you are ready to determine if the partnership will fulfill the expectations of the organizations and their leaders. If you plan to move forward, you must be willing to tie your successes to each other.

Finally, in the Perform Stage of Relationship Development, the hallmarks are high levels of trust and high-quality productivity. Again, if you are unwilling to tie your successes—and failures—to the future of the partnership, you will have a difficult time building the trust needed to sustain the partnership over the long haul.

Realigning the Six Partnering Attributes

Since the release of *Partnering Intelligence: Creating Value for Your Business by Building Strong Alliances,* we have had the privilege to work with hundreds of people and help them develop the skills to create strong partnerships. During this time, we have noticed that certain attributes help people accelerate through the Stages of Relationship Development. Thus, we have realigned the Six Partnering Attributes to the Stages of Relationship Development as follows.

Stages of Relationship Development	Partnering Attributes
Form	Self-Disclosure and Feedback
Storm	Self-Disclosure and Feedback Win-Win Orientation Ability to Trust
Norm	Self-Disclosure and Feedback Win-Win Orientation Ability to Trust Future Orientation Comfort with Change
Perform	Self-Disclosure and Feedback Win-Win Orientation Ability to Trust Future Orientation Comfort with Change Comfort with Interdependence

Applying the Stages of Partnership Development

In the following chapters we demonstrate how to implement the Stages of Partnership Development: Assess, Explore, Initiate, and Commit. Together they offer a successful, proven road map for creating partnerships. You will find yourself spending more time in the Assess and Explore stages because you will be determining your needs and looking for a partner who can help you satisfy those needs. By the time you're in the Initiate stage, you will be spending most of your time "doing" the task that the partnership was brought together to accomplish and less time nurturing and sustaining the alliance itself.

You can congratulate yourself if you move successfully into the final stage, Commit. You will have built the foundation of trust between the members of the partnership and you can then focus your attention on delivering the value proposition to the sponsors.

While some of the assessment steps might seem redundant, please don't short-circuit the process. Some of the most successful partnerships in the business world today were built using each and every step. This proven model is designed to allow each organization in a partnership to be in control of its own destiny and freely determine the needs and benefits the partnership offers. While it may take time to navigate the steps, it takes even longer to bail out of a broken partnership, pick up the pieces, and move on.

The business landscape is littered with broken partnerships. Don't let yours be one of them.

8

Assess Stage

Identifying What You Want from the Partnership

You're thinking about establishing an alliance. You know that there are areas of expansion, development, or expertise that you want to have access to and that the future of your business might depend on it. How do you go about determining if partnering to form an alliance is the right strategy? The answer to that question begins here, in the Assess Stage of Partnership Development (see Figure 7 below).

FIGURE 7

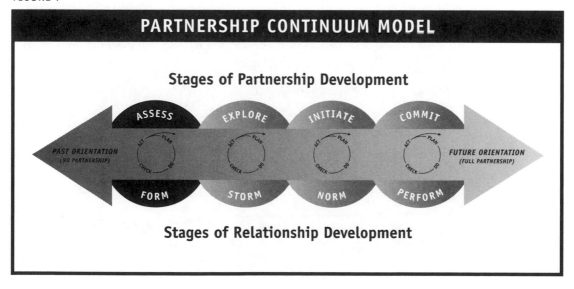

157

The Assess Stage: Are You Ready to Partner?

Establishing a partnership is an important organizational commitment that requires support from leadership down throughout the business. As a sage once said, "There are many ways up a mountain." In business, as in life, you have a range of options and strategies to help you attain your objectives. Partnering is one of the most important skills in business today and for the future, but it is not the only way to get business objectives met. Establishing a partnership means hard work and a commitment from leadership. Partnerships without this level of commitment are doomed to failure.

In this chapter on the Assess Stage of Partnership Development we introduce the following necessary steps:

- **Step 1:** Create the partnering team

- **Step 2:** Determine partnership readiness

- **Step 3:** Conduct an internal assessment

- **Step 4:** Identify partnership needs and objectives

- **Step 5:** Prepare a summary document

As you complete each of these steps, remember that you are also in the Form Stage of Relationship Development and that your key partnering attribute here is Self-Disclosure and Feedback. At the conclusion, you'll be ready to summarize your findings and identify future objectives.

Step 1: Create the Partnering Team

While most organizations discuss partnerships well in advance before forming them, it is still important to confirm the level of commitment. We recommend that this be done in a formal setting. Someone in the organization responsible for, and with the authority to create, the partnership should call the meeting. Typically, this might be a CEO, COO, or VP of business development. However, with internal partnerships, it could be from anywhere on the organizational chart, from a director to a team leader.

Establishing the "Home Team"

Being able to rely on support in a partnering situation is important to the success of the partnership. In internal partnerships, this means that functional or departmental leaders are working with each other to ensure success. In cross-functional endeavors, the outcome of the partnership might benefit one group more than another, yet everyone needs to be cooperative if the venture is to succeed.

For example, your proposed partnership might be between Engineering and Marketing, but the outcome primarily affects Sales. Engineering might not care about the marketing effort, but without Engineering support, Marketing can't advance a new product feature. Engineering may be more concerned about costs, since they are rewarded for staying within budget, and maybe the new feature development wasn't planned for this year. How do you ensure that Engineering and Marketing are working together to achieve both of their objectives? While partnering, both sets of leadership in Engineering and Marketing need to send the same message of support and priority. To do this, they become the "home team."

In external partnerships, those sponsoring the partnership and their key supporters become the home team for the group responsible for managing it. Having home team support is critical for building smart partnerships. When forming an external alliance, the two home teams come together. This is known as the partnering team.

Who Should Attend the Readiness Meeting?

We recommend that anyone who might be impacted by the project within the immediate organization attend the readiness meeting. That might mean executives, functional or departmental heads, or team representatives. These people will become the home team for the partnership. Regardless of whether it is internal or external, potential home team members should attend.

Referring to the completed sample below as a guide, use the Readiness Meeting Attendance Worksheet that follows to help you decide who should attend your initial meeting.

Sample Readiness Meeting Attendance Worksheet

Is this proposed partnership internal or external?

Internal alliance between Mkt. / Eng.

What groups in the company might the scope of this proposed partnership impact?

Marketing	Sales
Engineering	
Market Communications	

What level of authority do we need to form this partnership?

Vice President / Mktg. & Eng.

Who are potential "home team" members?

Mike S. / Eng.   Janice C. / Marketing   Jonah P. / Sales

What additional organizational input do we need to form this partnership? *(Check off the appropriate departments.)*

Human Resources_____Finance_____Information Technology ✓_____

Marketing ✓_____Sales ✓_____Customer Care ✓_____

Engineering ✓_____Market Communications ✓_____Legal_____

Public Relations_____ Distribution ✓_____Others_____

Who should attend the readiness meeting?

Mike S. / Eng.	Janice C. / Marketing	Jonah P. / Sales
Sandra / Info. Tech.	Mary W./ Market Comm.	
Jerry H. / Distribution	John R. / Customer Care	

What is the proposed readiness meeting date? May 6

Has an agenda been developed?   Yes / (No)

Readiness Meeting Attendance Worksheet

Is this proposed partnership internal or external?

_____

What groups in the company might the scope of this proposed partnership impact?

_____   _____

_____   _____

_____   _____

What level of authority do we need to form this partnership?

_____

Who are potential "home team" members?

_____   _____

_____   _____

What additional organizational input do we need to form this partnership?
  (Check off the appropriate departments.)

Human Resources_____Finance_____Information Technology_____

Marketing_____Sales_____Customer Care_____

Engineering_____Market Communications_____Legal_____

Public Relations_____ Distribution_____Others_____

Who should attend the readiness meeting?

_____   _____

_____   _____

_____   _____

What is the proposed readiness meeting date? _____

Has an agenda been developed?   Yes / No

Sample Partnering Readiness Meeting Agenda

Monday, May 6, Conference Room A

Purpose: To establish team readiness to form a partnership

Agenda: Introduction / Expectations / Housekeeping

Agenda Review

Overview of Proposed Partnership

Partnership Readiness Inventory

Discussion

Action Items

Next Steps

Pluses and Delta Session*

Time: 1:00–3:00 p.m.

---

*For a description of a "Pluses and Delta" session, see p. 167.

Preparing the Agenda

After you have decided who needs to attend the readiness meeting, you must put together an agenda similar to the sample shown above. Creating an agenda is important for several reasons:

• It identifies the purpose of the meeting

• It outlines the steps you'll take to accomplish the tasks proposed

• It sets up the time restrictions for accomplishing the tasks

• It keeps participants focused

We use a consistent format when creating meeting agendas. Consistency helps to build trust and confidence in others once it is demonstrated that keeping to the agenda helps accomplish objectives.

Step 2: Determine Partnership Readiness

The Partnership Readiness Inventory

The purpose of the Partnership Readiness Inventory is to facilitate the discussion about forming a partnership. While most of us readily believe we are good partners, we frequently focus on only one of the two dynamics of partnering. The Partnership Readiness Inventory is designed to get those responsible for sponsoring or creating the partnership to commit to its success by focusing on both the task and the relationship dynamics involved. It explores issues concerning trust, teamwork, vision, mission, and support of the partnership.

Action Step **Prepare to administer the Partnership Readiness Inventory on the following page. Note that it can be administered before the meeting or during the opening of the meeting. However, results of the survey need to be kept strictly confidential so people are comfortable answering honestly. No one should be forced to reveal or defend his or her responses to the inventory. Upon their completion collect all the Partnership Readiness Inventories. On a flip-chart, tally the scores for each question on the inventory.**

Once people have had the opportunity to see how the others have scored the inventory, move through each question and solicit comments and responses. With the exception of Question 1, if all the answers are in the "Yes" column, you are ready to partner. If Question 1 has a majority of "Yes" responses, you will want to ask the group why they are considering a partnering strategy. If there are more than two or three "No" responses to Questions 2–10, you must take the time to talk about the issues that have been identified. It is important to facilitate this in a safe and sensitive manner to be sure you don't create a win-lose outcome for individuals whose support you might need in the future.

PARTNERSHIP READINESS INVENTORY

Question	Yes	No
1. Could you satisfy all the requirements in the proposed partnership by yourself?		
2. Given your experience with individual team members, do you think you'll be satisfied with the way this team interacts?		
3. Is the organization's culture receptive to using the skills necessary to form strong partnerships?		
4. Does the organizational culture rely on past history to make decisions?		
5. Inside the organization, do individuals and departments work together to solve problems and issues?		
6. Do you believe everyone in the meeting is committed to forming a strong partnership?		
7. Do you know and understand the partnership's vision?		
8. Do you know and understand the partnership's mission?		
9. Do you know and understand the strategies involved for the proposed partnership?		
10. Are you satisfied that all the cross-functional agreements are in place to make this proposed partnership a success?		
Total Score		

Suggested General Debriefing Questions

After a group discussion on the Partnership Readiness Inventory, follow up with this general debriefing.

- What are your overall impressions of the scores from this inventory?

- What does this tell us about our readiness to partner?

- What strengths do you think we have as a team?

- In what areas do we need improvement?

- What do we need to do before establishing the partnership?

- What are our next steps?

Be sure to document all team agreements. Conclude with a Pluses and Delta session (see p. 167).

What If the Majority Say No?

What do you do if the majority of people answer "No" to one or more of Questions 2–10? The following exercise offers some suggestions on how you might want to debrief the meeting.

DEBRIEFING SUGGESTIONS	
Question	**Strategies for Proceeding**
1. Could you satisfy all the requirements in the proposed partnership by yourself?	• If the people in the meeting feel that they can satisfy all their business needs without partners, *ask:* "Why are you partnering?"
2. Given your experience with individual team members, do you think you'll be satisfied with the way this team interacts?	• *Ask:* "What were past issues or behaviors that prevented you from working together effectively?" • Make agreements on future behaviors
3. Is the organization's culture receptive to using the skills necessary to form strong partnerships?	• *Ask:* "What attributes will prevent the team from successful partnering?" • List the attributes for discussion and the roadblocks they'll cause • Develop a plan to move forward by addressing the roadblocks • Agree to periodically follow up
4. Does the organizational culture rely on past history to make decisions?	• *Ask:* "How will relying on past history help us move forward in a new partnership?"

Question	Strategies for Proceeding
5. Inside the organization, do individuals and departments work together to solve problems and issues?	• *Ask*: "How will our inability to work together effectively impact our partnership?" • "What messages will we send to partners?" • "What do we need to do to work better together internally?"
6. Do you believe everyone in the meeting is committed to forming a strong partnership?	• *Ask:* "What impact will not having everyone committed to the partnership have?" • "What issues are preventing commitment?" • "What do we need to do to build commitment?"
7. Do you know and understand the partnership's vision?	• Clarify or create a partnership vision statement
8. Do you know and understand the partnership's mission?	• Clarify or build a partnership mission statement
9. Do you know and understand the strategies involved for the proposed partnership?	• Clarify or build partnership strategies
10. Are you satisfied that all the cross-functional agreements are in place to make this proposed partnership a success?	• Identify cross-functional issues • Use Win-Win Orientation to negotiate agreements • Document the agreements

What's a "Pluses and Delta" Session?

A Pluses and Delta session is simply a way for you to gauge what worked for this meeting and what you would improve for the next meeting. It's a quick and uncomplicated method for gaining immediate feedback. On a flip-chart, draw a T bar. On its left side, put in a plus sign (+), and on the right side, draw a Delta sign (Δ), the Greek symbol for *change*. Then, going around the room, ask participants what worked for the session and what they would change for the next meeting. Below is a sample Pluses and Delta chart.

Meeting Pluses and Deltas

+	Δ
• Well-prepared	• Allow more time
• Got people to talk	• Provide snacks /drinks
• Honest	• Encourage people to stay until the end
• High level of participation	• Do this more often
• Good chance to get together	
• Got us thinking	

Home Team Roles and Responsibilities

Now that you've determined that you want to partner, you need to review team members' roles and responsibilities. The types of home teams you form will be determined by the roles they will play in the partnership. External partnerships typically have two levels of home teams, depending on the size and complexity of the alliance: (1) a sponsorship team, which is responsible for the strategic development of the partnership; and (2) a leadership team, which is responsible for the day-to-day operation of the partnership.

SPONSORSHIP TEAM

The sponsorship team usually resides at the executive level of an organization. They are the people who are responsible for the strategic development of the external partnership. Their responsibilities include the following tasks:

- Establish the organization's vision and mission for the partnership

- Determine the organization's strategic compatibility

- Understand the organization's current and future economic position

- Appreciate the strengths and weaknesses of the organization's culture

- Become aware of the organization's capabilities

- Conceptualize future strategic possibilities and alignment

- Know operational alignment and capability issues

- Advocate partnerships within the organization

- Secure resources for the partnership

- Establish both internal and external communications

- Establish external Partner Relationship Management (PRM) at a high level

- Maintain internal alignment and resource allocation

- Set priorities

LEADERSHIP TEAM

Typically, executive leadership is not directly involved in the day-to-day operations of the partnership. This is typically delegated to a leadership team that is responsible for implementing the partnership's objectives and overseeing the integration of work it is charged with doing. Several levels of staff may report to the managers of the operations. Their responsibilities may include the following tasks:

- Implement the sponsor's vision and mission for the partnership

- Develop organizational integration plans

- Develop the cultural and partnering capabilities of the people who will be working together

- Manage budget and growth

- Create strategies and tactics for partnership operations

- Build relationships between partnering team members

- Problem-solve using a Win-Win Orientation

- Continually build trust within the partnership

- Communicate with sponsorhip team on progress, concerns, issues

- Manage processes

- Communicate with partner's sponsorship team

- Look for new opportunities for growth

- Manage operational political issues

- Determine resource use

Integrating the Roles and Responsibilities into the Partnership's Culture

Integrating the responsibilities of the sponsorship and leadership teams into the culture of the partnership is important. The sooner you can communicate roles and responsibilities to the people working within the partnership, the less confusion and discord will occur. When people understand who is responsible for what, they are confident about moving ahead, knowing that if problems arise in the future, there is a clear path to follow for resolution.

Step 3: Conduct an Internal Assessment Using the Holistic Organizational Model

The purpose of conducting an internal assessment is to define your needs and to help you later in your search for the right partner in the Explore stage. Smart partners conduct internal assessments differently than most other organizations. They understand that knowing their strengths and weaknesses based only on their process capability provides a narrow insight into the organization. Since most partnerships fail due to relational issues, understanding your leadership styles and business culture is just as important as understanding your processes, if not more so. Conducting an internal assessment includes three important phases:

- **Phase One:** Understanding your strategic focus

- **Phase Two:** Building your strategic framework

- **Phase Three:** Knowing your processes

- **Phase Four:** Identifying capabilities and needs

We begin Step 3 by putting into context the purpose of these activities by using the Holistic Organizational Model. We then take the core elements of the model to create the Strategic Framework.

The Holistic Organizational Model

To explain the internal assessment process, we use the Holistic Organizational Model shown in Figure 8. This model consists of the two important "realms" that exist in all organizations: the ethereal and the material. The ethereal realm makes up the human spirit and energy of the organization. The material realm represents the output of that spirit and energy. Each has an important role to play in the success of the organization and the partnership.

The ethereal energies influence the types of relationships that are possible based on the leadership's vision, values, and ethics, which determine the spirit of the organization and help to define the cultural parameters of the business. These parameters help to establish the organization's norms of behavior and operational boundaries, in other words, the culture. The culture then dictates the paradigms that create the material outputs. Products and services result from specific strategies, tactics, and processes the business puts into place.

FIGURE 8

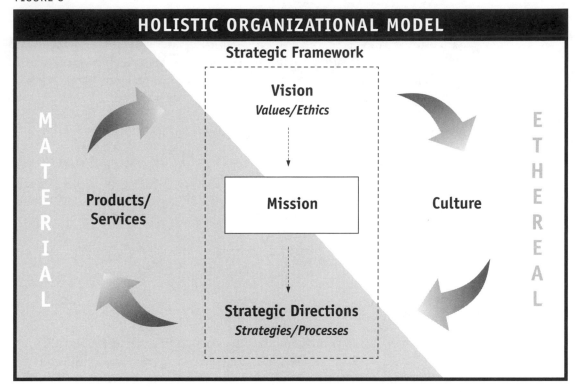

HOLISTIC ORGANIZATIONAL MODEL

Strategic Framework

Vision
Values/Ethics

MATERIAL

Products/ Services

Mission

Culture

ETHEREAL

Strategic Directions
Strategies/Processes

At the core of the Holistic Organizational Model resides the Strategic Framework. The purpose of the Strategic Framework is to link the vision with the strategic directions of the partnership. This is accomplished by defining the mission of the partnership, which is the keystone that connects the ethereal vision with the material strategies.

At the start of an internal assessment, you will want to make sure that your home team is in agreement about why you want to partner. Having them go through the process of creating a Strategic Framework will provide plenty of opportunity to have discussions and clarify questions that may arise, building internal ownership of the partnering process.

Alignment of the Ethereal and Material Realms

It is important that what the organization says it wants to do and what it does are in alignment. Internally misalignment results in decreased human energy and externally in mistrust. One way to prevent misalignment is to have strategic alignment between the vision and mission and the strategies you engage in to accomplish them. Therefore, after agreeing to partner, you will want to make sure that the sponsors of the partnership endorse your Strategic Framework—the vision, mission, and strategic directions in which the partnership will move.

Phase One: Identifying Your Strategic Focus

Before creating your Strategic Framework, however, you need to reflect on the "strategic focus" of your organization. This is important since your entire Strategic Framework is predicated in the proposition of the partnership, that is, what it is you want to have happen. The most common areas of strategic focus are:

- Satisfying customer needs

- Developing innovative new products and services

- Executing operational excellence

Businesses usually pick one strategic focus and excel in that area. For instance, FedEx excels in operational excellence, moving packages faster and cheaper than its competition. 3M is known for its product innovation. Nordstrom's is noted for its ability to provide customer satisfaction, no matter what the cost.

World-class organizations understand they cannot excel in all three areas. They focus on one of the three competencies and become a leader in that area. This does not mean they ignore the other two competencies. Rather, it means they may be "fast followers" or outsource those areas that do not support their core business competency. While some leaders may view this as a negative, it is actually important to understand where you want to focus and align your skills. This frees you to allocate resources toward the areas you choose and provides people with focus and guidelines when establishing priorities.

Action Step Have each team member answer the questions on the Strategic Focus Worksheet on the following page. Then, review and discuss each issue, come to an agreement on what your proposed partnership strategic focus needs to be, and complete the sentences following the weeksheet.

STRATEGIC FOCUS WORKSHEET

• What assumptions are you making regarding the market?

_____

_____

• What are your competitors doing or offering that is different?

_____

_____

• What are you doing to differentiate yourself in the market? List current strengths and weaknesses.

_____

_____

• What are your competitors' market strengths and weaknesses?

_____

_____

• What are the economic indicators that may impact your business?

_____

_____

• What consumer trends are occurring in your market?

_____

_____

• What synergies are happening with your current products or services?

_____

_____

• What type of market demographic information have you reviewed?

_____

_____

• Our primary strategic focus is (specify area):

_____

_____

• We will be "fast followers" in (specify areas):

_____

_____

Phase Two: Building Your Strategic Framework

The Strategic Framework comprises both the ethereal and material constructs within which the partnership will operate. It provides the organization the vision of the partnership, its mission, and the strategic directions the alliance will undertake in completing its objectives (see Figure 9 below).

This component of partnership development must be thoroughly analyzed by the sponsorship team. If you are a member of the leadership team, the Strategic Framework will be the most important guidance you will offer to the team of people who will be expected to implement the partnership's work.

FIGURE 9

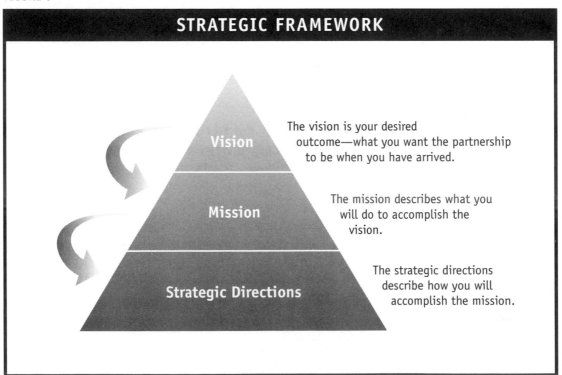

STRATEGIC FRAMEWORK

Vision — The vision is your desired outcome—what you want the partnership to be when you have arrived.

Mission — The mission describes what you will do to accomplish the vision.

Strategic Directions — The strategic directions describe how you will accomplish the mission.

Sample Strategic Framework

National Product Development Company (Manufacturing)

Vision

- To be the most innovative enterprise in our field and the preferred supplier in the products we manufacture

Mission

- Satisfy customers with superior quality, value, and service

- Provide investors an attractive return through sustained, quality growth

- Respect our social and physical environment

- Be a company employees are proud to be part of

Strategic Directions

- Support innovative and entrepreneurial research that satisfies our customers' needs

- Grow mutually beneficial relationships between our employees, customers, and the communities we live in

- Generate shareholder value through innovative products that are first in the marketplace and sustain value over time

---

Sample Strategic Framework

National Wireless Telephone Company (Service)

Vision

- Working together to make it easy for people to connect with their world without limits

Mission

- Achieve global leadership in delivering surprisingly simple wireless data and voice solutions

Strategic Directions

- Provide integrated solutions that meet customer data, voice, and network needs

- Be the first to furnish customers with wireless capability in data space

- Execute in a way that delights customers, excites employees, and ignites the community

The Importance of a Vision Statement

A vision statement forms a company's guiding force. It is also the guiding force of every partnership. While you may have some vague notions of what you want the partnership to accomplish, it is important that you and your partners agree on the vision, the fundamental purpose of the partnership's existence.

INTERNAL AND EXTERNAL PARTNERS

The process for creating a vision statement will be the same regardless of whether it is an internal or external partnership. However, with an internal partnership you need to do this exercise only once. With an external partnership you need to do it once with your home team, and then once again with the combined leadership of the external partnering team to create a mutually agreeable vision statement. The process for developing a vision statement is outlined on the following page. The process is the same for developing a mission statement.

The Importance of a Mission Statement

While the vision statement expresses the fundamental and altruistic outcome of the partnership, the mission is more pragmatic. The mission describes in general terms how the partnership will accomplish the vision. The mission statement reflects the strategic focus of the partnership and may spell out in specific terms the partnership's area of expertise, market focus, or product development or application.

INTERNAL AND EXTERNAL PARTNERS

The process for creating a mission statement is identical to the process for creating a vision statement. It is the same regardless of whether it is an internal or external partnership. However, with an internal partnership you need to do this exercise only once. With an external partnership you need to do it once with your home team, and then once again with the combined leadership of the external partnering team to create a mutually agreeable mission statement.

Developing a Common Vision/Mission Statement

1. Contact each member of the internal team or home team who will be sponsoring the partnership. (You may want to use the Readiness Meeting Attendance Worksheet on p. 161.)

2. Prior to coming to the meeting, have members write their own two- to three-sentence vision/mission statement for the partnership.

3. With everyone together in the room, have each member write their vision/mission statement on a flip-chart sheet of paper and read the vision/mission statement to everyone in the room.

4. Tape the flip-chart sheets of paper along the walls of the room so everyone can see them.

5. After everyone has read their vision/mission statements and these are all posted on the wall, have people go around and privately review them.

6. Ask members to identify common themes and words that emerge from the vision/mission statements. You might want to use a highlighter to mark them.

7. After you have highlighted the common themes and words, write them on a separate flip-chart.

8. Based on the common themes and words, facilitate the discussion to create sentences that capture the essence of what they describe.

9. Order the sentences into a final vision/mission statement. Do not spend a lot of time wordsmithing. If the team is unable to develop this within an hour or so, some other dynamic is at play. Ask for two or three volunteers to develop the vision/mission statement apart from the group and bring it back to the team for consensus.

10. Once the vision/mission statement has been agreed upon, you will want to share it with the greater organization for feedback and comments.

Creating Strategic Directions

After you have completed the vision and mission statements for the proposed partnership, think about how you are going accomplish them. When discussing your strategic directions, think about the strategic focus you agreed to earlier in the process.

Organizations develop strategies that enable the business to accomplish its objectives. For instance, if your objective is to increase sales, you might develop three specific strategies to meet that objective, such as the following:

- Strategy 1: Provide more product features based on customer requests

- Strategy 2: Increase distribution channels

- Strategy 3: Improve product quality

Each of those strategies may then have dozens of tactics that support accomplishing the strategy. And each of those strategies could result in a partnership to help you attain your goals. There is no right or wrong way to develop strategic directions. Each organization takes a unique approach based on its understanding of what a strategic direction is and how to formulate it.

Here is how we do it. First, we review the mission statement and think about the area of strategic focus. Then, we begin to brainstorm ideas that might help accomplish the goals. Then, we follow the process on page 179. By following this process you will quickly identify common themes and categories that can be easily distilled into strategic directions.

Developing Common Strategic Directions

1. Contact each member of the internal team or home team who will be sponsoring the partnership. (You may want to use the Readiness Meeting Attendance Worksheet on p. 161.)

2. Prior to coming to the meeting, have members write down three to five strategic opportunities based on the strategic focus of the partnership.

3. With everyone together in the room, have each member write their strategic directions on a flip-chart sheet of paper and read them to everyone in the room.

4. Tape the flip-chart sheets of paper along the walls of the room so everyone can see them.

5. After everyone has read their strategic directions and these are all posted on the wall, have people go around and privately review them.

6. Ask members to identify common themes and words that emerge from the strategic directions. You might want to use a highlighter to mark them.

7. After you have highlighted the common themes and words, write them on a separate flip-chart.

8. Based on the common themes and words, facilitate the discussion to create sentences that capture the essence of what they describe. Do not spend a lot of time wordsmithing. If the team is unable to develop this within an hour or so, some other dynamic is at play. Ask for two or three volunteers to develop the strategic directions apart from the group and bring them back to the team for consensus.

9. Order the strategic directions based on priority as set by the partners.

10. Once the strategic directions have been agreed upon, you will want to share them with the greater organization for feedback and comments.

Action Step Now that you have developed all three elements of your Strategic Framework, formalize the framework using the template below, identifying the vision, mission, and strategic directions you have agreed to. Review this with the people who are involved. You might post the framework in several prominent locations along with a pad of Post-it® Notes and request employees to offer feedback on it. Another common technique for soliciting feedback is to hold employee focus groups. Regardless of the method you use, gathering feedback and acknowledging that feedback is an important step in building employee ownership of the Strategic Framework.

STRATEGIC FRAMEWORK
Vision
Mission
Strategic Directions
1.
2.
3.

You have now completed the second phase of the internal assessment. You have a solid Strategic Framework in place to act as the bulwark of your decision-making and priority-selection processes.

Phase Three: Knowing Your Processes

Processes are how the strategies will be implemented. They are the actions that fulfill the strategy and meet the specific needs of the customer. The most successful organizations utilize process management. Process management is a business science that documents, measures, analyzes, and improves business processes.

START BY UNDERSTANDING YOUR CORE BUSINESS PROCESSES

Core business processes comprise the types of work your business is engaged in: the products or services for which your customers pay you. Most businesses have some common processes at the macro level. The following sample core business model includes four processes, each with several subprocesses.

Action Step Referring to the sample below, label your core business processes in the template that follows. Then list the subprocesses that support your core business model.

SAMPLE CORE BUSINESS PROCESSES

1. Identification of Customer Requirements

2. Product/ Service Development

3. Marketing and Sales

4. Customer Service

Subprocesses:	Subprocesses:	Subprocesses:	Subprocesses:
1.1 Survey customer needs	2.1 Design product	3.1 Develop market plan	4.1 Bill customer
1.2 Identify market trends	2.2 Test product	3.2 Develop sales channels	4.2 Answer customer questions
1.3 Summarize customer requirements	2.3 Prepare for production	3.3 Distribute product	4.3 Collect customer feedback
	2.4 Manufacture product		

CORE BUSINESS PROCESSES

1.	2.	3.	4.

Subprocesses: **Subprocesses:**   **Subprocesses:**   **Subprocesses:**

_____   _____   _____   _____
_____   _____   _____   _____
_____   _____   _____   _____
_____   _____   _____   _____
_____   _____   _____   _____
_____   _____   _____   _____

In our example, "Summarize customer requirements," the output of sub-process 1.3, would then move to Product/Service Development, which would then create a product or service to satisfy those consumer demands. They would hand their output off to Marketing and Sales. Ultimately, Customer Service would invoice and collect the payments and answer any questions. They may also collect consumer feedback and give it back to the people involved in 1, "Identification of Customer Requirements."

As part of your internal assessment, you need to understand your core business processes to determine your business strengths and weaknesses. You can then use this information in helping to select a potential partner in the Explore stage (described in the following chapter).

Phase Four: Identifying Capabilities and Needs

Rating your process capabilities is also important in understanding what you need to be looking for in a strategic partner. For example, are you good at processing payments but lousy at servicing products? Do your strengths lie in marketing products, as you haven't developed a new product in twenty years?

Action Step To help you determine your areas of strength and weakness, complete the following Process Capability Rating Sheet to get an updated view of your capabilities. Distribute it to people inside your organization and, if you are comfortable with it, to your customers. This should help you identify the areas of concentration for your needs assessment.

PROCESS CAPABILITY RATING SHEET

Process	Excellent	Average	Poor	Comments
1. How well do we currently identify and design products to meet our customers' needs?				
2. How well do we currently design new products that are "hits" in the market?				
3. How effective are our marketing efforts?				
4. How would you rate our sales force efforts?				
5. How would you rate our billing services?				
6. How would you rate our follow-up service?				

Organizations that commit to this self-assessment process know their leadership style, articulate their visions for the future, and devise strategies and processes to realize that future. Here's where a critical assessment emerges. To get to where we want to go, do we use resources we already have, do we acquire it, or do we need to partner with other entities? Completing this exercise will help answer these questions.

The next step is to conduct a needs assessment. By now you should have a good understanding of your organization's focus. The next question you will be asking is "What do I need from a potential partner?" The steps for conducting a needs assessment are as follows:

1. Contract with participants.

2. Conduct your research.

3. Conduct data analysis.

4. Give a leadership presentation.

5. Ask for interpretation and conclusions.

6. Develop an action plan for next steps.

Action Step **Referring to the completed sample as needed, conduct a needs assessment using the template that follows.**

SAMPLE NEEDS ASSESSMENT

Step	Issue	Outcome	Recommendation
Contract with Participants • Identify team leadership • What leadership expectations come from your assessment? • Areas of focus for assessment task/relationship/both • Roles and responsibilities • Budget	No marketing representative Roles unclear None	 Team meeting to clarify roles CEO to fund project	• Identify needs assessment team • Expect a complete recommendation on partnering • Find a distribution partner
Research • Methodology to be used, such as surveys, interviews, focus groups, or questionnaires • Research objectives • Population or scope of assessment • Time	Time to collect internal information Needs to be completed quickly	Use online questionnaire	• Survey customers • Use internal questionnaire • Identify indirect market opportunities • Consumer markets • June 5-20, 2002
Data Analysis • Types of data – Qualitative – Quantitative • Content analysis • Categories	Can we get competitive data?	Use a third-party polling service	• Use both qualitative and quantitative data • Use existing product categories

SAMPLE NEEDS ASSESSMENT (CONTINUED)

Step	Issue	Outcome	Recommendation
Leadership Presentation • Provide leadership with data • Gain leadership validation of data • Get feedback from data	Who will lead the discussion?	Needs assessment sponsor agrees to lead the discussion	• Establish feedback date • Plan meeting • Complete presentation media
Interpretation/Conclusions • Ask leadership what data means to them • Provide insights into meaning of data • Gain leadership agreement on data interpretation	Need a prepared Q & A sheet	Team facilitator will provide	• Review leadership feedback • Incorporate suggestions • Ask for leadership support
Plan for Action • Gain leadership commitment to move ahead • Prioritize critical areas for action • Develop action plans for areas with high priority • Identify organizational impact • Focus on ethereal and material realms • Continue to use PDCA cycle*	Who speaks for leadership team? How do we get department heads to own action plans?	Sponsor will request CEO to speak for team Arrange for department head to be on action plan committees	• Get verbal OK to proceed w/ partnership • Get leadership team to prioritize action items • Get vice president's departmental impact statements • Build in PDCA after every meeting

*The Plan–Do–Check–Act cycle: see pp. 242–44.

NEEDS ASSESSMENT TEMPLATE

Step	Issue	Outcome	Recommendation
Contract with Participants • Identify team leadership • What leadership expectations come from your assessment? • Areas of focus for assessment task/relationship/both • Roles and responsibilities • Budget			
Research • Methodology to be used, such as surveys, interviews, focus groups, or questionnaires • Research objectives • Population or scope of assessment • Time			

Data Analysis
 	
• Types of data
  – Qualitative
  – Quantitative
 	
• Content analysis
 	
• Categories			

NEEDS ASSESSMENT TEMPLATE (CONTINUED)

Step	Issue	Outcome	Recommendation
Leadership Presentation • Provide leadership with data • Gain leadership validation of data • Get feedback from data			
Interpretation/Conclusions • Ask leadership what data means to them • Provide insights into meaning of data • Gain leadership agreement on data interpretation			
Plan for Action • Gain leadership commitment to move ahead • Prioritize critical areas for action • Develop action plans for areas with high priority • Identify organizational impact • Focus on ethereal and material realms • Continue to use PDCA cycle*			

*The Plan–Do–Check–Act cycle: see pp. 242–44.

After performing your needs assessment, you need to complete two more steps before moving into the Explore Stage of Partnership Development.

Step 4: Identify Partnership Needs and Objectives

At this point, you will want to document your needs and objectives toward the process of moving forward in finding a partner and meeting business goals. To better illustrate this important step, we will begin to build a partnering scenario for your sample company.

Action Step **Referring to the completed sample on page 190 as needed, complete the Partnership Needs and Objectives Worksheet template that follows. The sample assumes that you have completed your needs assessment and that you and your sponsorship team have agreed that you:**

- Need better follow-up on customer service

- Need a more complete understanding of consumer buying habits and trends

- Need a faster product development cycle

- Need more presence in major department store chains

The worksheet also helps you and your team determine:

- Types of actions you want to take

- Objectives you want to achieve

- Methods for measuring success

- Timeframe for actions

SAMPLE PARTNERSHIP NEEDS AND OBJECTIVES WORKSHEET

Strategic Focus	Need	Action	Objective	Measurement	Time
Understanding future consumers' buying habits and trends	More complete understanding of consumer buying habits	Partner with national market research company	Develop up-to-date profile of buying habits; complete by Q4	Greater variety of sales distribution channels Q2 – 2003	Interview research firms by 3/30
	Better follow-up customer service	Work with telemarketer to provide follow-up call	Call each new customer within 2 weeks of purchase	Increased % of customers called from 35-80%	Negotiate with telemarketer by 4/15; contract and script ready by 6/15
Increasing product development	Faster product development cycle	Increase product development staff by 5 people	5 new products annually	# of new products annually	By 4/15
Developing marketplace presence	More presence in major department stores	Establish department store partnerships	Increase product distribution in 3 new department stores	Two new stores by 12/30; one the following year	Identify candidates by 3/30; qualify by 6/30; final selection 10/30; contracts signed by

SAMPLE PARTNERSHIP NEEDS AND OBJECTIVES WORKSHEET						
Strategic Focus	Need	Action	Objective	Measurement	Time

Step 5: Prepare a Summary Document

The summary document is not one document but the compilation of all the components you've assembled during the Assess stage. Think of it as an "executive summary" of the Assess stage. The summary document is used both internally to help you identify the types of partnerships you want to pursue and also externally when approaching potential partners. These are the items you will want to discuss with them to identify how each partner can satisfy needs and negotiate the win-win outcome.

> **Action Step** **Develop a summary document that encapsulates your findings. The summary document should include whatever quantitative and qualitative data you've collected. You'll also need to write a summary paragraph. Identify your strengths and weaknesses, then document your needs. To assist you in preparing your summary document, complete the exercise that follows. Completing this checklist will ensure you've covered all the important items in your summary document.**

SUMMARY DOCUMENT CHECKLIST

Item	Completed?	Action Needed
Vision statement		
Mission statement		
Strategic directions		
Partnering strategies		
Work process analysis		
Organizational strengths		
Organizational weaknesses		
Needs assessment		
Can offer potential partners		
Objectives		

SUMMARY

Let's review some of the skills you've learned in this chapter.

Stage of Partnership Development—Assess Stage

- **Establishing the internal readiness to partner**

- **Creating a partnering team,** including the sponsorship team and the implementation team

- **Conducting an internal assessment** to your current situation, including: the ethereal realm, your vision, values, ethics, mission, and culture; and the material realm, your strategies, tactics, processes, products, and services. Understand the gap between your vision and the current situation and be ready to close that gap.

- **Identifying your needs** that you want a partner to help you satisfy and areas of competencies that you can offer to a potential partner

- **Summarizing your findings** in a document that you can give to potential partners

- **Identifying objectives** that you need to meet

Now it is time to move into the Explore stage of partnership development and identify potential partners.

9

Explore Stage
Identifying Potential Partners

The Explore stage is the time to identify potential partners and determine if the right mix of ethereal compatibility and material gains exists. During this stage partners should disclose their individual needs and identify the areas of win-win. Finding the right partner is critical to success. Once you've found the right partner, it's important to review your Strategic Framework to be sure you're aligned with each other's objectives.

As shown in Figure 10 below, this is the period during which you will most likely encounter the Storm stage of relationship development. As trust begins to form, you and your partners are more apt to test boundaries, causing conflict. This is when you and your partners will need to use your Win-Win Orientation and Ability to Trust skills.

FIGURE 10

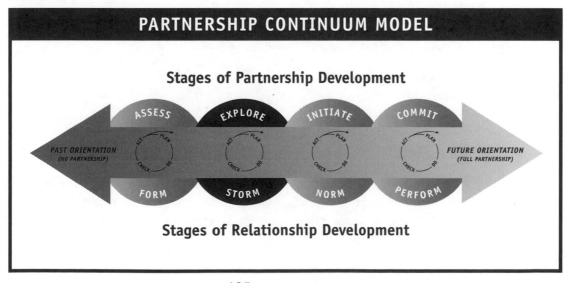

195

In this chapter, we will explore the following steps:

- **Step 1:** Identify potential partners

- **Step 2:** Identify and establish potential partners' needs

- **Step 3:** Develop areas of Win-Win Orientation

- **Step 4:** Create a joint Strategic Framework for the partnership

- **Step 5:** Formulate a partnering agreement

- **Step 6:** Plan an initial activity

Before continuing with these steps, however, let's review your needs and purpose for forming a new partnership.

Why You Need Potential Partners

Armed with the needs assessment you created in the last chapter, you are prepared to go looking for potential partners. You should now know:

- Your strengths and weaknesses

- Your needs

- Areas of focus for a strategic partner

This is the time to think about your overall purpose in forming your partnership. Typically, organizations form partnerships for one, or more, of the following three key strategic reasons:

- To increase product and service development and capability

- To increase distribution of product or service

- To increase competency level

Increase Product and Service Development and Capability

In a rapidly changing, increasingly sophisticated marketplace, consumers are demanding more selection and product features than ever before. Companies need to keep pace by bringing to market new products, services, or features that meet consumer demand. To do this, they may find it necessary to form partnerships with technology development, research, or other manufacturing companies. For example, GM partnered with Verizon Wireless to provide its OnStar service, offering a variety of services to subscribers of that product. GM needed a wireless carrier to make the system work, and Verizon obtained thousands of additional users on its network. Both win!

Increase Distribution of Product or Service

The ability to expand the scope of a product or service distribution is critical for organizations that are growing. The expense and difficulty of starting up new distribution channels are often prohibitive, especially when moving into the global marketplace. Establishing partnerships to increase distribution and develop new opportunities is often the easiest and most effective way to expand marketplace presence. An example of this is Amazon.com, which has partnered with FedEx to get product to customers in a hurry without the investment or hassle of running a delivery service.

Increase Competency Level

New products and services frequently require new skills and competencies. While one can hire or acquire those competencies, in this age of specialization it is often impractical to do so. Partnering with people who have those competencies may be a more effective way to go. Bank of America wanted to enable its human resource transactions to be accessible on the Web. Knowing that its core competency is in financial management, it partnered with Exult, a Web-based human resource firm, to build and manage the operational portions of its human resource organization. Bank of America was free to focus on its core business competencies, and Exult not only gained a new client, it was also given the opportunity to expand the scale of services needed to meet the payroll of an organization with 150,000 associates.

When you know you need partners to achieve your business goals, you can begin the process of identifying them.

Step 1: Identify Potential Partners

Step 1 includes four rounds:

- **Round One:** Brainstorm potential partners and establish partnering criteria

- **Round Two:** Conduct a needs-based selection process focusing on the results of your needs assessment

- **Round Three:** Establish potential partner priority

- **Round Four:** Select and prioritize potential partners based on your partnering criteria

Round One: Brainstorm Potential Partners and Establish Partnering Criteria

Bring together your partnering team. On a flip-chart, brainstorm as a group and think of as many potential partners as you can. You may want to conduct some informal research beforehand.

For the purpose of this exercise, we will use the information provided in the Sample Needs Assessment and the Sample Partnership Needs and Objectives Worksheet in Chapter 8. These samples helped identify three areas of potential partnerships for your sample company:

- A national market research company

- A department store

- A small manufacturer

Let's say you have decided to focus on a national market research company. First, brainstorm as many national research companies as possible. You may want to do some research to gather the names of potential partners. This helps you to get to know who's available. Your sample company selected the following potential partners:

- Elderson Marketing Research, Minneapolis, MN

- Consumer Research Company, Minneapolis, MN

- IQ Research, St. Paul, MN

- AC Nielsen, Chicago, IL

- Business Information Technologies, Denver, CO

- Focus Market Research, New York, NY

Once you have identified your list of potential partners, you will need to establish the criteria you will use to rank them. In this case, the partnering criteria your sample company established are as follows:

- Strategic fit

- Cultural fit

- Process fit

- Subject matter

- Geographic location

- Previous or current relationships

Each criterion is ranked high (H), medium (M), or low (L) relative to its impact in the selection process, with comments noted.

Action Step Referring to the completed sample as a guide, complete the Criteria Ranking Sheet that follows.

SAMPLE CRITERIA RANKING SHEET

Partnering Criteria	Impact	Comments
1. Strategic fit—Can they satisfy our needs?	H	Willing to review
2. Cultural fit—Can we trust them and work well together?	H	Must trust information and data collection methodology
3. Process fit—Are our work processes compatible?	M	Our systems are flexible
4. Subject matter—Are they experts in the areas we are exploring?	H	Must have expertise in Millennium Generations preferences
5. Geographic location—Are they close enough for personal contact?	M	The closer the better
6. Previous or current relationships—Have they successfully partnered in the past?	L	Nice to have, but not necessary

CRITERIA RANKING SHEET

Partnering Criteria	Impact	Comments
1.		
2.		
3.		
4.		
5.		
6.		

Once you have completed this exercise, you are ready to begin your selection process.

Round Two: Conduct a Needs-Based Selection Process Focusing on the Results of Your Needs Assessment

Your next task is to differentiate between the strengths of the prospective partners you identified in the brainstorming process.

Action Step **Referring to the completed sample as a guide, complete the Needs-Based Selection Matrix template that follows, based on the results of the needs assessment you conducted in Chapter 8. Fill in the areas of strength you bring to a partnership and areas of weakness that you need a partner to help you improve. Put an *X* next to those items you think you can help a potential partner with *and* next to those items you believe a particular partner can help you with.**

SAMPLE NEEDS-BASED SELECTION MATRIX

Company	We Offer (Strengths)				We Need (Weaknesses)				
	National Presence	Attractive Demographics	More Business Opportunities	Potential Billing Capabilities	Valid Market Research	Trend Data on Millennium Generation	Feedback on Products	Suggestions on New Designs	Suggestions on New Features
Elderson Marketing Research, Minneapolis, MN		X	X		X		X	X	X
Consumer Research Company, Minneapolis, MN	X					X			
IQ Research, St. Paul, MN	X		X	X	X	X	X	X	X
AC Nielsen, Chicago, IL					X	X	X	X	X
Business Information Technologies, Denver, CO		X		X	X				
Focus Market Research, New York City, NY	X		X		X		X	X	X

Completing this exercise will help you gain an idea of who your best potential partners might be based on your internal best knowledge. This is yet untested data, and you will want to be more rigorous in your selection process in the following phases.

NEEDS-BASED SELECTION MATRIX

Company	We Offer (Strengths)				We Need (Weaknesses)				

WHAT DOES THE MATRIX TELL US?

To analyze potential partners, you will want to review the criteria. Are they still valid? With the team, discuss each of the rankings. In our sample case, on first blush it would appear that Elderson Marketing Research would be a prime candidate. However, on closer examination, we see they are not specialists regarding trend data for the Millennium Generation, a key demographic group for the product. Consumer Research Company may not offer the same business opportunities (though that is still an unknown), but they do have trend data on the Millennium Generation. AC Nielsen and Business Information Technologies each have the capacity to satisfy all your needs but are not in an ideal geographic location. IQ Research appears to have the best fit so far.

Round Three: Establish Potential Partner Priority

Your next step is to begin prioritizing your partners.

> **Action Step** Referring to the completed sample as a guide, complete the Selection Grid of Potential Partners using the template that follows. List your selection criteria along the top and your potential partners down the left-hand side. With your team using its best insights, rank each potential partner high (H), medium (M), or low (L) against the selected criteria. Convert your rankings into numerical scores using the scoring grid at the bottom.

Completing this exercise yields two important outcomes. The first involves the discussion that you and your team will have while ranking potential partners. You can explore assumptions and share information you have about them. This helps your team clarify its expectations for the partnership. The other important outcome involves the ranking of potential partners based on your best perceptions of them. The aim is to satisfy your needs while meeting a set of criteria you've established as necessary for success.

SAMPLE SELECTION GRID OF POTENTIAL PARTNERS

Partnering Criteria

Company	Strategic Fit	Cultural Fit	Process Fit	Subject Matter	Geographic Location	Previous/Current Relationship	Total Score
Elderson Marketing Research, Minneapolis, MN	L (1)	H (5)	M (3)	L (1)	H (5)	L (1)	16
Consumer Research Company, Minneapolis, MN	L (1)	L (1)	L (1)	H (5)	H (5)	L (1)	14
IQ Research, St. Paul, MN	M (3)	H (5)	H (5)	H (5)	M (3)	H (5)	26
AC Nielsen, Chicago, IL	M (3)	L (1)	M (3)	H (5)	M (3)	L (1)	16
Business Information Technologies, Denver, CO	M (3)	M (3)	H (5)	H (5)	L (1)	L (1)	18
Focus Market Research, New York City, NY	L (1)	M (3)	M (3)	L (1)	L (1)	M (3)	12

Scoring the Selection Grid

High (H) = 5 points
Medium (M) = 3 points
Low (L) = 1 point

SELECTION GRID OF POTENTIAL PARTNERS

Partnering Criteria (substitute as necessary)

Company	Strategic Fit	Cultural Fit	Process Fit	Subject Matter	Geographic Location	Previous/Current Relationship	Total Score

Scoring the Selection Grid

High (H) = 5 points
Medium (M) = 3 points
Low (L) = 1 point

Note that on the sample selection grid, the priority established for contacting potential partners would be:

1. IQ Research
2. Business Information Technologies
3. AC Nielsen / Elderson Marketing Research: tie
4. Consumer Research Company
5. Focus Market Research

Round Four: Select and Prioritize Potential Partners Based on Your Partnering Criteria

Now you will want to test your priority selection to ensure that you have identified a partner that can not only satisfy your needs, but meet your criteria as a partner as well.

Action Step Referring to the instructions below and the completed sample as a guide, complete the Selection & Criteria Analysis Grid template that follows.

1. Enter the partnering criteria from the Criteria Ranking Sheet (p. 200) you completed earlier.

2. Combine the criteria rankings (H, M, or L in the "Impact" column on p. 200) and your selection ranking from your Selection Grid of Potential Partners (p. 205), in that order.

3. Score the ranking combinations based on the table below. *Please note:* Ranking scores are weighted to give highest priority to criteria important to you.

High–High	= 12 points
High–Medium	= 8 points
High–Low	= 1 point
Medium–High	= 8 points
Medium–Medium	= 8 points
Medium–Low	= 1 point
Low–High	= 4 points
Low–Medium	= 2 points
Low–Low	= 1 point

SAMPLE SELECTION & CRITERIA ANALYSIS GRID

Partnering Criteria

Company	Rank	Strategic Fit	Cultural Fit	Process Fit	Subject Matter	Geographic Location	Previous/Current Relationships	Total Score
		H	H	M	H	M	L	
IQ Research		H–M (8)	H–H (12)	M–H (8)	H–M (8)	M–M (8)	L–H (4)	48
Business Information Technologies		H–M (8)	H–M (8)	M–H (8)	H–H (12)	M–L (1)	L–L (1)	38
AC Nielsen		H–M (8)	H–L (1)	M–H (8)	H–M (8)	M–M (8)	L–L (1)	34
Elderson Marketing Research		H–L (1)	H–H (12)	M–H (8)	H–L (1)	M–M (8)	L–M (2)	32
Consumer Research Company		H–L (1)	H–L (1)	M–L (1)	H–H (12)	M–M (8)	L–L (1)	24
Focus Market Research		H–L (1)	H–L (1)	M–H (8)	H–L (1)	M–L (1)	L–M (2)	14

SELECTION & CRITERIA ANALYSIS GRID

Partnering Criteria (substitute as necessary)

Company	Rank	Strategic Fit	Cultural Fit	Process Fit	Subject Matter	Geographic Location	Previous/Current Relationships	Total Score

PRIORITIZING POTENTIAL PARTNERS

Based on the rankings in the Sample Selection & Criteria Analysis Grid, IQ Research is the top candidate for a potential partnership for your sample company. Of course, at this point you have no idea if they are interested in partnering with you. You have three other candidates that, while not ideal, could make good partners. You will probably rule out Focus Market Research, as they rank lowest in the analysis by a sizeable margin.

ESTABLISHING CONTACT

You now have your list of potential candidates. You are going to want to put some thought into how to contact and initiate a discussion with them to determine interest. Here are some guidelines to follow:

1. Research each organization and identify the CEO, CFO, president, or anyone involved in strategic partnerships.

2. Determine each company's reputation, economic viability, stock value, and trends.

3. Get to know the organization's products, services, and distribution channels.

4. Interview their customers, if possible, and their employees, if this can be done discreetly.

5. Determine if they have had any other partnerships or alliances. How did they work?

Learn as much about your potential partners as you can before meeting with them. This will help you in three ways:

1. When developing a partnering strategy, you will have data to help you determine whether or not this organization can meet your needs.

2. Getting a feel for the organization's culture will help you determine whether you are compatible.

3. Spending time getting to know your partner and their business sends an important message to them that they are important and you're serious.

Once you have made contact, establish a date to meet, preferably in person. Pick a natural location such as their office or, better yet, suggest they name the meeting place. The key is to put them in a comfortable spot and give them as much control over the environment as possible.

It is important to be honest and direct about what it is you want at the initial meeting. To do this, you will want to be prepared. Bring whatever documentation you have and plan to share it with them.

START WITH THE STRATEGIC FRAMEWORK

Show them your Strategic Framework—your vision, mission, and strategic directions. Explain what you are trying to accomplish and why. Ask for feedback. This is the perfect time to demonstrate your Self-Disclosure and Feedback skills.

Tell them about your needs assessment—your strengths and weaknesses. Expound on your strengths and explain why your weaknesses are hindering your progress toward achieving your vision. They need this information to help determine if they want to partner with you. Don't be shy about talking about your weaknesses. Partners have the uncanny ability to pick them up quickly anyway. You can't hide them.

MAKE THE PROPOSAL

After you have had a chance to break the ice about what you want, ask them if they are interested in exploring the potential of partnering with you. Don't be surprised if they don't know. Based on the level of the people you're meeting with, they may need to go back to their organization and have discussions with leadership. Here's a list of what to do at the initial meeting:

- Ask them to think about your ideas

- Give them copies of your Strategic Framework and other documentation as needed

- Ask them if they have a partnering model they use to develop partnerships; if they have one, ask to see a copy of it

- If not, show them your model and explain the process to them

- Tell them that if they want to pursue the partnership, you would like them to conduct their own internal needs assessment to determine what they might need from a partnership with you and to document their strengths and weaknesses

- Ask them to develop their own Strategic Framework for partnering—vision, mission, and strategic directions—as a starting point for discussions

- Offer to help them in any way you can, since you have gone through the process and can provide insights into how to work it

- Set a date to meet in the future

The ball is now in their court. They have to decide if partnering with you is something that would benefit them. Remember, people and partners do things for their own reasons, not yours!

Step 2: Identify and Establish Potential Partners' Needs

After you've found interested potential partners, it's time to identify needs and determine if you share a mutual vision. This is a critical part of the process. You will need to build on your Self-Disclosure and Feedback skills to make sure that you and your potential partners are exploring every facet of your needs and expectations.

Identifying and establishing partners' needs includes two rounds:

- **Round One:** Agree on the nature of your relationship

- **Round Two:** Identify the "value proposition"

Each round is designed to ensure not only that value for the partnership exists, but that you can build the kind of trustworthy and mutually beneficial relationship that will allow the partnership to flourish.

Round One: Agree on the Nature of Your Relationship

Why are you forming the partnership? Is it to:

- Increase product and service development and capability?

- Increase distribution of product or service?

- Increase your competency level?

- Improve operational capability?

Different organizations may form partnerships for different reasons. For example, you may be partnering with a specialized manufacturer to increase product development, and they may need your distribution channel to increase marketplace presence. As we've developed it, your sample company needs both information about market trends to design more up-to-date products and market research to focus on the right market segments for your products.

IQ Research wants to move into the hard market (manufacturing) and be less reliant on their current area of soft-market expertise (fashion). To do that, they need access to hard-market consumers, which you can provide. You can also offer insights into technological innovation in your area of manufacturing.

Business Information Systems already offers hard-market data and therefore has access to the consumers they need for research. They would like to have access to your technological innovations, however.

An analysis after meeting with your two most likely partners indicates a strategic fit for both potential partners. However, IQ Research has more needs you can satisfy than does Business Information Systems and therefore a higher potential for partnering success.

Action Step Referring to the sample as needed, complete the Key Strategic Areas for Partnership exercise for the partner you are considering, using the template that follows.

SAMPLE KEY STRATEGIC AREAS FOR PARTNERSHIP

Partners	Increase Product Development	Increase Distribution	Increase Competency
Your Company	Market trends		Market research
IQ Research	Transition from soft market to hard market data	Access to consumers	Technology trend information
Business Information Systems			Technology trend information

KEY STRATEGIC AREAS FOR PARTNERSHIP

Partners	Increase Product Development	Increase Distribution	Increase Competency

Round Two: Identify the "Value Proposition"

A key element to any partnership is the ability to identify and extract the value of the partnership. The additional value the partnership generates—whether in increased competencies, revenue, product enhancement, or distribution—is called the value proposition of the partnership. This is enhanced when synergy exists between the parties. The old adage 1+1>2 is important when defining the value proposition. You will want to think about value from three different perspectives as shown in the sample below.

- **Economic value:** Direct increase in revenue or savings due to partnership

- **Marketplace value:** Enhanced marketplace value of product or services such as features or benefits due to the alliance

- **Operational value:** Cost savings from enhanced efficiencies due to partnership

The key to moving toward a strategic partnership is identifying the value proposition beyond the obvious. It doesn't take genius to understand that if you mix a candy bar with ice cream you will increase sales and both suppliers will benefit. However, when the partners look beyond the obvious and begin to explore other opportunities, partnerships flourish, becoming more strategic and interdependent.

SAMPLE VALUE PROPOSITIONS	
Area of Value Proposition	**Example**
Economic value	A bank invests millions of dollars into a technology-based human resource outsourcer to enhance their capability and capacity. Computer manufacturer shares development cost with camera company to offer video-on-demand service.
Marketplace value	Big-brand candy company works with ice cream manufacturer to blend products and increase sales for both.
Operational value	Auto manufacturer partners with big-name designer to enhance image and prestige of car. Nationwide cellular service partners with auto company to provide wireless services to owners of luxury cars.

For example, the bank and human resource outsourcing case above appears straightforward on the surface. However, the genius of the partnership becomes apparent when you look at the secondary benefits. The human resource company wanted to demonstrate to future clients that it could handle large-scale organizations. After partnering, it could provide testimonials from a prestigious national bank with more than 150,000 employees all doing human resource transactions online. The bank, whose core business is focused on financial solutions, is positioned with the human resource company to manage payroll transactions for their clients. That means millions of dollars of new business being managed by the bank, thanks to the partnership.

The chart below illustrates how our sample business can approach identifying the value proposition. Based on this analysis, you would benefit in both the economic and marketplace value areas. IQ Research would benefit in all three areas, and Business Information Systems would benefit in the operational value area only. It appears that there is still a good strategic fit between you and IQ Research.

Action Step Referring to the sample below as needed, complete the Value Proposition Identification exercise that follows for the partners you are considering.

SAMPLE VALUE PROPOSITION IDENTIFICATION			
Partners	Economic Value	Marketplace Value	Operational Value
Your Company	Opportunity for savings in product development	Enhanced reputation as a "trend-setter"	None
IQ Research	Opportunity for savings through being provided a readymade base of consumers and information	Opportunity to expand into hard-market research	Access to new technological innovation, which saves developmental cost
Business Information Systems	None	None	Access to new technological innovation, which saves developmental cost

VALUE PROPOSITION IDENTIFICATION			
Partners	Economic Value	Marketplace Value	Operational Value

Now that you have identified the areas of value proposition, determine if you have similar visions for the partnership.

Step 3: Develop Areas of Win-Win Orientation

Determining the value proposition enables you to move forward into identifying and developing specific areas of Win-Win Orientation. There are two rounds involved in this process:

• **Round One:** Brainstorm potential areas of Win-Win Orientation

• **Round Two:** Prioritize and agree on areas of Win-Win Orientation

Round One: Brainstorm Potential Areas of Win-Win Orientation

GENERATE IDEAS

With your partners in the room, begin the *generation* stage of brainstorming. In this stage, the purpose is to generate as many potential ideas as you can. Think outside the box! Think wild and crazy ideas! List as many as you possibly can.

CLARIFY IDEAS

In the *clarification* stage, you go through your list of ideas and clarify them to ensure that everyone in the room understands what the ideas mean. Typically, most ideas will be self-explanatory, but some may be fragments or labels that become clear only when an explanation is provided by the idea's owner. Write any clarifying statements on the list to be sure nothing is lost.

CATEGORIZE IDEAS

You will probably find that some ideas can fit into some specific category with other ideas. In the *categorize* stage, you put together similar concepts and build categories of ideas. This helps to narrow down and organize areas of collaboration and mutual interest.

Round Two: Prioritize and Agree on Areas of Win-Win Orientation

The purpose of this round is to identify the priority each partner puts on each category, using a Priority Matrix. This exercise helps partners see the importance of each other's issues.

SCORING THE PRIORITY MATRIX

Your team and your partner's team should meet separately to score the Priority Matrix. Within the team, scoring the matrix can be approached in two ways:

Individual Scoring with Team Average—Preferred Method

In this method, each member of the team scores the Priority Matrix individually. Once that is completed, you can list the individual scores and calculate a team average. During the process, it is important to ask clarifying questions about why people scored the way they did. Once you've completed the scoring individually and have a team average, rank the items in importance. It is key at this point to validate the ranking. You need to ask, "Do we all support the ranking? Is this what we really want to move forward with?" Once those questions are answered to everyone's satisfaction, you are now ready to meet your potential partners to see how *they* prioritized the matrix.

- Advantage of this method: Each individual has equal input without outside influence

- Disadvantage of this method: Unless there is complete discussion on the final ranking, and unless consensus is achieved, the average score may not be the most strategically important priority. Therefore, you should avoid basing your decision strictly on an average score. It needs to be done in conjunction with consensus agreement.

Team Consensus—Secondary Method

Using this method, the team discusses each item and through the process comes to an agreement on its priority.

- Advantage of this method: It increases the opportunity for discussion and building consensus as a team

- Disadvantage of this method: Some people may feel pressured to score one way or another or defer to stronger team members, losing valuable perspectives and input

Action Step Referring to the sample below as needed, complete the Priority Matrix that follows. Use a simple scale of 1 to 5, with 1 being lowest priority and 5 being highest priority.

SAMPLE PRIORITY MATRIX				
Opportunity	Your Company	IQ Research	Total Score	Scale Ranking
1. Merging consumer market data-bases	3	5	8	3
2. Developing new technology for gathering market trend data	2	5	7	4
3. Developing a jointly owned market research company focused on the Millennium Generation and their technology needs for the future	4	5	9	2
4. Developing a product development think tank	5	5	10	1
5. Creating a strategy to move into new marketplaces based on consumer demographics	5	1	6	5
6. Sponsoring joint teen expositions to gather their ideas on what they want from technology	5	5	10	1

PRIORITY MATRIX

Opportunity	Your Company	Partner	Total Score	Scale Ranking

BRING THE TWO TEAMS TOGETHER

Once each of the partnering teams has individually scored the Priority Matrix, you now can share your scores. On a flip-chart, draw the Priority Matrix and have each team write in their scores. Then rank the items.

This is the time for discussion. What do you think? What do they think? What surprises you? Are you in agreement, or are there vast differences in how you scored? You now have the opportunity to demonstrate your ability to put three of the Six Partnering Attributes to work:

- Self-Disclosure and Feedback

- Win-Win Orientation

- Ability to Trust

SELF-DISCLOSURE AND FEEDBACK

This is the time for open and honest dialogue on whether or not you can get your needs met in this partnership. In your drive to find a Win-Win Orientation, you've put your business on the table. Are you going to get your needs met in this Priority Matrix, and is your partnering business going to get its needs met?

WIN-WIN ORIENTATION

If you both have scored and ranked the items similarly, that's great. It means you've probably done a good job up-front in understanding your needs and finding a partner who has a complementary set of needs. But what if the scores are vastly different? How do you reconcile the differences? Here is where you couple your Self-Disclosure and Feedback skills with your ability to find win-win solutions.

ABILITY TO TRUST

You must also be convinced that your potential partners are trustworthy enough to help you all get to the Win-Win Orientation. This might be a good time to talk about trust in the relationship. Go back to Chapter 4 and review some of the components of the Ability to Trust. Talk about them with your partners. This will set the stage for meaningful dialogue to help find win-win solutions.

Once you have identified the Win-Win Orientation and opportunity between the partners, you are ready to develop the partnership's Strategic Framework. This is an exciting time for the partnership—having a common vision, mission, and strategic direction will give the partnership its structure and purpose.

PARTNER COMPATIBILITY ANALYSIS

You've had a chance to meet your potential partners and to score your priorities in the partnership. This is an ideal time to do a quick compatibility exercise.

Action Step **Complete the following Partner Compatibility Analysis, answering questions about your partner. Have your partner complete the same analysis for you. Then share the analyses with each other. This exercise is a good way to foster discussion about whether or not you feel there is enough compatibility to continue the discussion and develop a joint Strategic Framework.**

PARTNER COMPATIBILITY ANALYSIS

Question/Answer	Compatible? Yes/No	Comment/Actions Needed
What is partner's vision? **Answer:**		
Where do they want to go as a business? **Answer:**		
What are their values and ethics? **Answer:**		
What kind of corporate culture do they have? **Answer:**		
What types of relationships and partnerships do they now have? **Answer:**		
How well have they been working? **Answer:**		
What are their strategies to achieve their vision? **Answer:**		
Have they conducted an internal assessment? **Answer:**		

Step 4: Create a Joint Strategic Framework for the Partnership

Have each group create its own Strategic Framework of vision, mission, and strategic directions, as outlined in Chapter 8 (with a template on page 180). Then bring the leadership of the teams together to develop a *joint* Strategic Framework.

Why Do We Need a Joint Strategic Framework?

A Strategic Framework agreed upon by both partners is essential to the partnership's success. A joint Strategic Framework is necessary to:

- Ensure alignment between partners on the scope and scale of the partnership

- Get agreement on how the vision will be accomplished via the mission statement

- Stimulate discussion, identification, and resolution of issues early in the process

- Help partners to think about their relationship with each other and where they want it to go

- Provide a formal venue for discussing strategies

- Elevate the level of discussion from tactics to implementation

- Get agreement on a decision-making framework for future opportunities

The joint Strategic Framework is more than just a document defining the vision, mission, and strategic directions of the partnership. It is a structure that forces partners to discuss the possibilities and roadblocks the partnership may face in the future. More important, it is a time for relationships to be built, to get to know each other as people, to understand each other's dreams and aspirations, and to build trust among the partners.

Communicating Your Needs

When you have defined the joint Strategic Framework, think about understanding each other's needs. This process is best conducted in a formal setting, with partners sitting in a room, facing each other, and talking through the questions provided. This takes time. Be sure to allow about four hours to meet. The following exercise will help you organize the session and clarify your needs.

COMMUNICATING YOUR NEEDS WORKSHEET

Question	Your Response	Partner's Response
1. Based on your vision of the partnership, what do you need from your partner?		
2. Strategic needs: What do you expect from your partner from a strategic perspective?		
3. Are there any areas that are off-limits? What are they?		
4. Based on your mission of the part-nership, what do you need from your partner?		
5. Tactical needs: What do you expect your partner to do?		
6. How do you expect resources to be managed?		
7. How will you make decisions about the priorities of projects?		
8. How do you follow up to ensure implementation?		
9. Relationship needs: What is your expectation about trust between the partners?		
10. How would you like to measure the level of trust between partners?		
11. What level of communication do you expect?		
12. With whom and how frequently?		

COMMUNICATING YOUR NEEDS WORKSHEET (CONTINUED)

Question	Your Response	Partner's Response
13. How do you expect to be given feedback?		
14. How do you prefer to give your partner feedback?		
15. Is there a structure for communication?		
16. What does a win-win situation look like to you?		
17. How do you expect decisions will be made between you?		
18. What happens when you can't agree?		
19. How do you expect your partner to manage change?		
20. How do you expect your internal team to manage change?		
21. How will you manage leadership issues?		
22. What level of communication do you expect with the sponsorship team?		
23. Objectives: What ideas do you have for establishing strategic objectives?		
24. How would you measure them?		
25. What ideas do you have for establishing tactical objectives?		
26. How would you measure them?		
27. What ideas do you have for establishing relationship objectives?		
28. How would you measure them?		

Step 5: Formulate a Partnering Agreement

We'd like to think that once we've agreed to partner with another organization, it's smooth sailing from that point forward. Perhaps that's true in a perfect world, but unfortunately this isn't a perfect world. Consequently, it's important to document all agreements between partners, both as reference for the future and as historic documentation. Following is an example of a partnering agreement.

Partnering Agreement

ARTICLE I   DECLARATION OF POLICY

This section is used to describe the purpose of the partnership and may include its goodwill expectations, vision, and mission.

ARTICLE II   DEFINITIONS

This section defines terms such as the following to clear up any ambiguous assumptions:
- Partnership
- Win-Win Orientation
- Value Proposition
- Conflict Resolution
- Trustworthiness

ARTICLE III   SCOPE OF AGREEMENT

This section identifies what the agreement applies to, the terms for the life of the partnership, and the areas in which the partnership will be working.

ARTICLE IV   CONDITION OF THE PARTNERSHIP

This section sums up the conditions of the partnership, which may include agreements such as:
- Access to information
- Strategic directions
- Performance indicators
- Financial contributions and resource allocations
- Timelines
- Shared resources
- Exiting strategies and trigger points

Partnering Agreement (continued)

ARTICLE V RELATIONSHIP EXPECTATIONS AND AGREEMENTS

This section describes expectations of relationship activities and may include:
- Decision-making and escalation processes
- Conflict resolution processes
- Relationship indicators
- Trust building
- Levels and frequency of communication
- Leadership issues
- Problem-solving methodology
- Number of meetings, and when and where

ARTICLE VI GOVERNANCE PROCESSES

This section discusses how the partnership will operate from a governance perspective. It may cover such issues as:
- Partnership metrics and milestones
- Leadership team structure, roles, and responsibilities
- Operational team structure, roles, and responsibilities
- Governance protocols and processes
- Alliance management objectives and goals

ARTICLE VII METHODOLOGY FOR WORKING TOGETHER

This section describes such issues as:
- Partnership project methodology
- Oversight and supervision
- Change management processes
- Management of partnership and projects
- Roles and responsibilities

ARTICLE VIII EFFECT OF AGREEMENT

This section affirms that by signing the agreement, both partners agree to the terms of the agreement.

ARTICLE IX SUCCESSOR CLAUSE

This section describes what will happen if either partner is sold or is acquired by a third party.

Signatures: _____

Date: _____

Step 6: Plan an Initial Activity

One of the biggest pitfalls in creating a partnership is that partners rush to reap the rewards of their hard work too fast. After the partnership is agreed to, they try to accomplish everything at once. Rather than trying to "boil the ocean," start with one high-priority project on your list and use it as a test project. Test it to see how well you work together and how the relationship evolves as the task is accomplished.

This provides the partnership with two significant advantages. The first is that it allows the relationship to develop under more normal conditions. Why risk putting the relationship into a pressure cooker? By starting with a single project, you can take the time needed for planning, allowing the relationship to develop on its own.

The second advantage is that starting small ensures that your processes are compatible. Often when working in partnership, one team does a part of a process and the other team does another part. The partnership may quickly discover that processes don't always integrate as smoothly as they'd hoped. Before moving full steam ahead, you'll have the opportunity to work out the bugs, making sure things operate smoothly when you do press forward.

In the example we've been following, your partnership has determined its top priorities. As an initial activity, you decide to sponsor joint teen expositions to gather teens' ideas on what they want from technology. Then, based on that input, you develop a joint product think tank to come up with product ideas to bring to market. This helps both sets of partners. Your company needs data on the Millennial Generation trends, and IQ Research wants to move from the "soft market" of fashion into the "hard market" of manufacturing.

This demonstates a true Win-Win Orientation. Conducting a teen exposition provides an easy, low-risk way to kick off the partnership and give it an early win.

Planning the Initial Activity Together

You already know what your top priority is. You will now want to start the planning process with your partners to implement the project.

The key to success is to plan the implementation of the project together. This is the first test for the partnership, and it is also the first opportunity to demonstrate that trust and mutual benefits can be attained. You will want to agree on a single project plan for both teams. Having one project will reduce confusion and add to the efficiency in completing the project.

Balance the Task with Relationship Issues

When planning the initial project, you can use the time-management scheme depicted in Figure 11 below, which balances the initial task with relationship building. During the first trimester, spend about 80 percent of your time discussing and agreeing on how you are going to work together, and about 20 percent of your time on the actual project task. Once you've determined how the relationship will work (review your partnering agreement in Step 5 above), spend the next trimester at about 50 percent on the task and 50 percent ensuring the relationship is still building trust and is mutually beneficial.

In the last trimester, because you have built a foundation of trust and demonstrated the benefits, you are poised to spend 80 percent of your time devoted to the task and 20 percent to relationship maintenance. While you may think you are losing ground on accomplishing the task by devoting so much time initially to relationship building, you are, in effect, investing in a more productive and efficient team. You will be amazed at how this investment in relationship building will reduce misunderstanding, conflict, rework, and defects because you have worked the relationship issues out in advance.

FIGURE 11

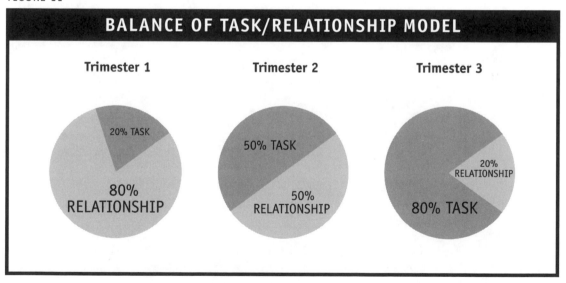

BALANCE OF TASK/RELATIONSHIP MODEL

Trimester 1 — 20% TASK / 80% RELATIONSHIP

Trimester 2 — 50% TASK / 50% RELATIONSHIP

Trimester 3 — 20% RELATIONSHIP / 80% TASK

Agree on Project Indicators and Measurements in Advance

As part of the initial project plan, be sure to agree on the indicators and measurements in advance. Make sure that your agreement includes:

- **What you will measure:** define it

- **When you will measure:** agree on data collection periods

- **How you will measure:** agree on data collection methodology

- **How you will analyze the data:** agree on the meaning of the data

- **What plan of action will be taken** if the project falls short of goals or targets that are set

- **What your improvement methodology will be**

SUMMARY

Let's review what you have accomplished in this chapter.

Stage of Partnership Development—Explore Stage

- **Identifying potential partners**—you identified the strategic areas you needed to partner in and established partner criteria and needs-based selection processes

- **Identifying and establishing partners' needs**—you had a preliminary meeting with potential partners to determine receptivity and agreed on the strategic nature of the partnership

- **Developing areas of win-win**—you determined the value proposition of the relationship and priority of potential projects the partnership would engage in. You and your potential partner agreed that it is a compatible relationship.

- **Creating a joint Strategic Framework**—you developed a mutual vision, mission, and strategic direction for the partnership

- **Formulating a partnering agreement**—you documented the agreements of the partnership, both task and relationship

- **Planning an initial activity**—you worked together to develop a plan to implement and determined that the value proposition and relationship issues will work

In the next chapter, we cover how to communicate and organize in the Initiate stage to bring the partnership to life.

Initiate Stage
Communicating and Organizing for Project Success

You have found a partner. You've formed a partnership and you've developed a plan to build a trustworthy and mutually beneficial relationship. You have planned an initial activity, something that is a priority for the partnership, and now you need to follow through on it. It's time to determine through your work on this task if this partnership is right for you, as you move into the third stage of partnership development, Initiate, as shown in Figure 12 below.

FIGURE 12

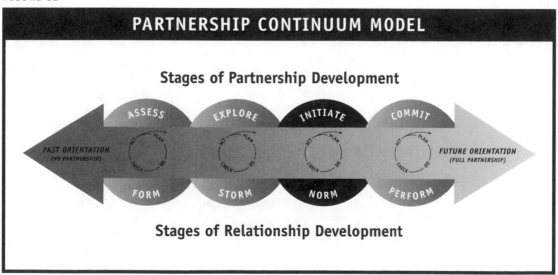

231

In this chapter, you will undertake the following steps:

- **Step 1:** Review the Six Partnering Attributes

- **Step 2:** Utilize a project management checklist

- **Step 3:** Communicate the plan within and between organizations

- **Step 4:** Check progress on both tasks and relationships

- **Step 5:** Use the PDCA cycle for successful outcomes

Step 1: Review the Six Partnering Attributes

Are your partners doing what they said they would do? Do you trust what they are saying to others about your project? Do they revert back to "their way" of doing things? You've worked hard on tasks. Now is a good time to focus again on the relationship.

The Six Partnering Attributes are the skills and behaviors that create the culture of the partnership. In Part One of this fieldbook, you reviewed the Six Partnering Attributes individually. You strived to increase your PQ, or Partnering Intelligence. How do the Six Partnering Attributes relate to the work you're doing now? They support the four Stages of Relationship Development, as shown below in Figure 13.

FIGURE 13

STAGES OF RELATIONSHIP DEVELOPMENT

Form ⟹	Storm ⟹	Norm ⟹	Perform
Self-Disclosure and Feedback	Self-Disclosure and Feedback	Self-Disclosure and Feedback	Self-Disclosure and Feedback
	Win-Win Orientation	Win-Win Orientation	Win-Win Orientation
	Ability to Trust	Ability to Trust	Ability to Trust
		Future Orientation	Future Orientation
		Comfort with Change	Comfort with Change
			Comfort with Inter-dependence

Regardless of expertise, educational level, or experience, these partnership stages occur within typical human cycles that over time help people build trust and ensure mutual benefits in their relationships.

Activities Checklist Exercise

Action Step Have each member of the partnering team complete the Activities Checklist that follows and share responses with the group. If there are significant differences in how team members respond, determine the core issues causing the differences. List each issue in the "Issue" column. Then, using Win-Win Orientation, agree on a resolution to any differences.

ACTIVITIES CHECKLIST				
Question	My Response	My Partner's Response	Issues	Resolution
1. Are you doing what you said you were going to do? **(Ability to Trust)**				
2. Are we spending time finding balance between task and relationship issues? **(Task/Relationship Balance)**				
3. Are you feeling trust between us? **(Ability to Trust)**				
4. How are we adapting to the changing situation? **(Comfort with Change)**				
5. Are we resolving conflicts and solving problems using win-win solutions? **(Win-Win Orientation)**				
6. Are you acting independently of us or are we in true partnership?				

Question	My Response	My Partner's Response	Issues	Resolution
7. Do you feel like we clearly understand what you want and need in the partnership? **(Self-Disclosure and Feedback)**				
8. Are you open to receiving feedback? **(Self-Disclosure and Feedback)**				
9. Do you feel like we are sharing information? **(Self-Disclosure and Feedback)**				
10. Are we planning for the future or reverting to past habits? **(Future Orientation)**				
11. Are we making decisions together? **(Comfort with Interdependence)**				
12. Are we forming new mental maps on how we work together? **(Future Orientation)**				
13. Do you trust your partner to complete tasks? **(Ability to Trust)**				

Step 2: Utilize a Project Management Checklist

Project management involves juggling a number of tasks, physical and mental. Besides giving a start-to-finish direction, completing a project management checklist helps you perform an analysis of all the options and gives you a way of checking flaws that might be fixed before it's too late.

Action Step After sharing responses in the above exercise and resolving differences, the entire team can review project plans using the following 25-question checklist.

PROJECT MANAGEMENT CHECKLIST

Question	Yes/No	Comments
1. Is there a business problem to be solved or a business opportunity to exploit?		
2. Is the measure of performance defined?		
3. Are the high-level achievements defined?		
4. Are the scope and assumptions defined?		
5. Have you prepared a preliminary risk analysis?		
6. Have you received the necessary formal and informal project plan approvals?		
7. Have you identified the project team?		
8. Have you made revisions or added detail to the measure of performance, high-level achievements, scope, assumptions, and risks with the project team as necessary?		
9. Have you completed a breakdown of the project's work processes?		
10. Is the communication system defined and in the plan?		
11. Do you have project governance in place?		
12. Are the performance contracts for the project team and stakeholders defined and agreed upon?		
13. Is the project team functioning appropriately?		
14. Do you know the current status of your project clearly?		
15. Are all project team members and stakeholders appropriately apprised of the project status?		

PROJECT MANAGEMENT CHECKLIST (CONTINUED)

Question	Yes/No	Comments
16. Is the project completed or terminated?		
17. Are all reports, inspections, evaluations, and communications complete for project closure?		
18. Do you have your Plan–Do–Check–Act (PDCA) cycle in place for project improvement?		
19. Do you have an exit strategy in place should the project not produce the desired results?		
20. Have you shared your partnering model?		
21. Have you built up your Self-Disclosure and Feedback skills?		
22. Are you working on attaining win-win solutions to conflicts and problem solving?		
23. Have you reviewed project team trust issues? Do you have a change management model in place that the whole team is comfortable with?		
24. Have you talked about new ways of completing the project vs. using old methodology?		
25. Are personal and team rewards in place that support and foster interdependence?		

Step 3: Communicate the Plan Within and Between Organizations

After the plan has been approved and you have reviewed all aspects of your project, you will want to communicate the plan to people within all affected organizations. Be creative about how you communicate the partnership. You might want to do the following activities:

- Hold a kick-off celebration

- Create press releases or conduct a press conference

- Broadcast on the Internet

- Include the plan in company publications

- Hang banners

- Design joint logos

- Create joint advertisements

You are now starting to implement the initial activity. You have invested time in the relationships and are spending most of your time on project tasks. This does not mean that you forget the relationship issues. You must periodically verify that trust is being built into the partnership and mutual benefits are being achieved.

Step 4: Check Progress on Both Tasks and Relationships

Once the initial activity or project is close to completion, you will want to debrief with the entire team to review the initial activity as well as relationship issues.

Action Step Complete the Debrief from Initial Activity exercises that follow to determine how well initial tasks were accomplished and to assess relationship building in the partnership.

DEBRIEF FROM INITIAL ACTIVITY—TASKS

Debrief Question	Response
What was the outcome of the first activity?	
Did you accomplish what you expected?	
Did the project plan work as expected?	
What did you learn from the activity?	
What surprised you about the activity?	
Did your planning provide the information you needed to determine the mutual benefits?	
What breakthrough occurred through working in partnership?	

DEBRIEF FROM INITIAL ACTIVITY—RELATIONSHIPS

Debrief Question	Response
Did you find balance in the task and relationship components?	
How did you cope with the change the initial activity created?	
Did you build trust? How do you know?	
How did you manage conflict?	
Can you give specific examples of conflict that were resolved using a win-win solution?	
Did the partners create a sense of interdependence? Did you rely on each other for success?	
How did you do in self-disclosure?	
Did you give your partner feedback? Did you receive feedback?	
How did the flow of information work?	
What type of information was shared between the partners?	
Did the information sharing create any breakthroughs in working on the project?	
Did something new and completely different happen that you didn't expect? What was it?	

After debriefing you may want to take stock of both your personal trust level and the trust level of the partnership.

 **Action Step** **Complete the Personal Trust Level Survey that follows to assess your own trusting capabilities in the partnership.**

PERSONAL TRUST LEVEL SURVEY

Directions

Circle your rating for each statement.   1 = Never   2 = Rarely   3 = Sometimes   4 = Often   5 = Always

Statement

1. General Trust In general, I am a trusting person.	1	2	3	4	5
2. Self-Confidence I trust myself to get the job done if that's what I've promised to do.	1	2	3	4	5
3. Trusting Another Specifically, with _____, I feel my trust level is very strong.	1	2	3	4	5
4. Situational Point of View I am less concerned about my past dealings with _____ than with what we will do from now on.	1	2	3	4	5
5. Willingness to Confront My Partner I feel comfortable demanding accountability from my partner.	1	2	3	4	5

Action Step   Now bring the partnering team members together again to individually complete the Trust Questionnaire for Partners exercise that follows. Have each team member fill out a copy and hand it in anonymously. Score the total results of the survey on a flip-chart sheet. Discuss the results of the survey with the group. Have you built trust or damaged trust? Make sure to keep your initial results on hand, as you will be revisiting this questionnaire in the next chapter.

TRUST QUESTIONNAIRE FOR PARTNERS

Directions
Circle your rating for each statement.   1 = Never   2 = Rarely   3 = Sometimes   4 = Often   5 = Always

Statement

1. I feel a high level of trust in this partnership. Why?	1	2	3	4	5
2. There is a high level of trust between the members of this partnership. Why?	1	2	3	4	5
3. I believe the partnership helps me get my needs met. Why?	1	2	3	4	5
4. I believe I help my partners get their needs met. Why?	1	2	3	4	5
5. It is easy for me to express my needs to my partners. Why?	1	2	3	4	5
6. I believe my partners trust me. Why?	1	2	3	4	5
7. I believe I behave in a trustworthy manner. Why?	1	2	3	4	5
8. I believe my partners behave in a trustworthy manner. Why?	1	2	3	4	5

Step 5: Use the PDCA Cycle for Successful Outcomes

The success of any partnership is determined by what is actually accomplished, not what was intended or possible. As we define the expectations of each other related to a task, we also define the expectations we have of each other in the relationship. We talk about our relationship in terms of behaviors we think are acceptable, mainly promising to come through on future performance. We also agree in a collaborative spirit to hold each other accountable. This involves our own style of Win-Win Orientation. If you're not happy with the way I'm performing a promised task, what will you do about it? How will you and I communicate?

Rather than just hope that the partnership delivers what it is capable of achieving, we use a structured process that helps control the partnership outcomes more effectively. It's unrealistic to assume that all partners know how to meet each others' expectations without addressing both task and relationship issues ahead of time. Knowing about certain cycles that repeat in relationship processes can help us communicate to achieve successful outcomes.

Think about how you plan an outing or vacation. Like most people, you usually plan a vacation in advance. You decide where you're going, where you're staying, and what you want to do. Then you go and do it. You come home and consider how well the vacation met your expectations. Was Acapulco as great as you had heard it was? Did Germany live up to what you had hoped it would be? If the vacation met your expectations, you might decide to return to your destination; if not, you'll pick some other place. This simple process is called the Plan–Do–Check–Act (PDCA) cycle (see Figure 14).

It is important to note that the PDCA cycle is as useful in developing relationships as it is in managing tasks. We use this simple tool repeatedly throughout the partnering process. Following is a comprehensive explanation of the PDCA cycle.

1. Plan

The first step in the PDCA cycle involves deciding what actions we should take to accomplish a task. Breaking down a manufacturing, sales process, or performance procedure into its parts is not hard to do. We also need to plan our relationship. We need to discuss and identify those components of the relationship we agree are important. These include the nature of the rela-

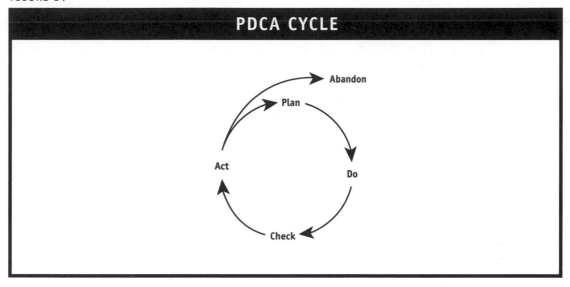

FIGURE 14

PDCA CYCLE

tionship and how we'll resolve conflicts, make decisions, and communicate. Like the logical steps in accomplishing a task, these preparations can lead to an open, constructive relationship. In the partnership, whether we're working on a task or the relationship, we need to agree on our plan.

2. Do

After we agree to a plan, we carry it out. We accomplish the plan by solving problems, making decisions, and communicating as we had planned to do.

3. Check

Did we follow our plan? Did we end up where we thought we would? Did the relationship work out? The phrase "reality check" is popular in business discussions today because often we seem to become so wrapped up in activity that we forget to step back and see how we're doing. In this step, we should simply observe how well we've implemented our plans, and then consider what new information we need to improve the partnership.

4. Act

Our reality check should reinforce the effectiveness of our process or help us understand at what point our process has broken down. We can learn to improve our planning. We can recommit to executing our plan better. Perhaps we should evaluate more frequently. What can we improve? How can we do better? What's the best decision we can make in the moment? In this step, we study the results of our processes, draw conclusions, and decide how we will act in the future to improve our relationship.

The "A" in our PDCA cycle could also mean that the action we take is to *abandon* the activity. We might discover we do not work well together. This is the perfect time to acknowledge that fact before we have too much invested in the partnership. Companies frequently find that their cultures or technologies are not as compatible as they thought they might be. Rather than continuing down a path that will lead nowhere, it's sometimes best to look for a new partner. This is a healthy sign of maturity and growth for all parties involved. As with dating, you learn something about your partner and, just as important, you learn something about yourself. You have just increased your Partnering Intelligence. If after the initial activity the partnership does not achieve the expectations and needs of all parties, it's an appropriate time to quit and move on.

5. Plan Again

Based on what we've learned, we're now smarter and better able to incorporate new learning into the next phase of the PDCA cycle. Now we can re-enter the cycle with a new plan, new knowledge, and a better opportunity for success. Acquiring Partnering Intelligence is a continuous learning cycle that we use in every phase of the partnering process. The PDCA cycle is a framework to help you forge better partnerships.

To work further with the PDCA concept, use the PDCA Action Plan to ensure that each activity you are engaged in provides you with the opportunity to learn what has worked and what you need to do better next time. Refer to the sample as needed in completing this exercise.

SAMPLE PDCA ACTION PLAN

Activity	When	Measurement	Outcome	Improvement
1. Develop meeting date and agenda	By June 30th	Did I meet the date?	2 days late	Enlist Admin. to help
2. Get meeting facilities arranged	By July 6th	Did I meet the date?	Met	No change
3. Send out meeting invitations	By July 8th	Did I meet the date?	I day late	Allow 3 days instead of 2 to print invitations
4. Hold meeting within budget	After Aug 20th	Assigned budget $5,000		
5. Meet participants' expectations	After Aug 20th	Meeting feedback sheets		

PDCA ACTION PLAN

Activity	When	Measurement	Outcome	Improvement
1.				
2.				
3.				
4.				
5.				

SUMMARY

Let's review some of the skills you've learned in this chapter.

Stage of Partnership Development—Initiate Stage

- **Reviewing your project plan** with all partners and their sponsors

- **Utilizing a project management checklist**

- **Communicating the plan** within and between organizations

- **Checking progress** on both task and relationship areas using a structured methodology

- **Using the PDCA cycle** for continual improvement

In the next chapter, "Commit Stage," we learn how committing to a partnership brings long-term value to all partners.

Commit Stage
Moving into Full Partnership

Everything you have done up to this point has been focused on getting you to this final stage, Commit, in which you commit to a full partnership, as shown in Figure 15 below. You have navigated the first three Stages of Partnership Development to ensure that trust and mutual benefits are present. You have used the PDCA cycle to continually improve both task and relationship dynamics of your partnership, and you have studied the Six Partnering Attributes to increase your PQ. You have seen the cultural orientation of the partnership move from a past orientation to a future orientation.

FIGURE 15

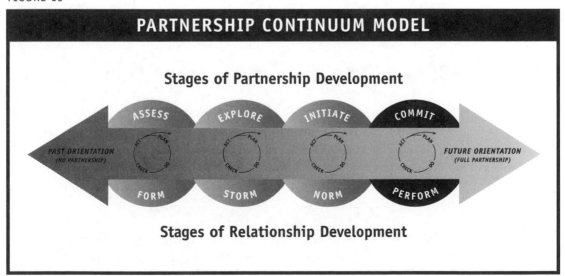

After all that work, this final stage may feel anticlimactic. This is a good thing. Preparing to make a commitment to the partnership should feel like a natural and logical next step. Once you have made the commitment to partnership, the only thing that stands between you and full partnership is being willing and able to conduct a joint strategic planning session to solidify your future vision and cement the plans to get you there.

From a relationship perspective, the partnership is now is the Perform Stage of Relationship Development. You have achieved the trust and communication needed to maximize the synergy of the partnership. You have identified the mutual benefits that the partnership promised. You have managed the changing dynamics of the relationship and their impact on the organizations.

In the Commit stage you will be taking the following steps:

- **Step 1:** Determine the level of commitment

- **Step 2:** Develop a joint strategic plan

- **Step 3:** Move to full partnership

Reaching this stage of partnership development is like winning the gold medal of partnering. It is the altruistic stage, when self-conceptualization can transform "me" to "we." You have moved from independence to interdependence as you link your successes to each other's well-being.

This goal has been elusive for most business partnerships. Changing business needs, evolving marketplace realities, and shifting priorities challenge even the strongest long-term relationships. Achieving this level of partnership will ensure that as long as trust exists and the partnership provides mutual benefits, successful outcomes will result. The partnership becomes solid and stable when there is formal recognition and commitment to it.

Step 1: Determine the Level of Commitment

One of the first things you will do as you move toward full partnership is verify that trust has been built between the partners. We have emphasized the importance of measuring trust throughout the Initiate stage. Now it's time to determine if this partnership has built trust. Because trust is such an important ongoing component of a successful partnership, it's important to assess your feelings about it again.

> *Action Step* **On the next page retake the Trust Questionnaire for Partners. Compare the results to your completed questionnaire on page 241 to gauge how the trust level has evolved. If there are signs of a decreased trust level, you need to discuss this with your partner.**

TRUST QUESTIONNAIRE FOR PARTNERS (REVIEW)

Directions

Circle your rating for each statement.   1 = Never   2 = Rarely   3 = Sometimes   4 = Often   5 = Always

Statement

1. I feel a high level of trust in this partnership. Why?	1	2	3	4	5
2. There is a high level of trust between the members of this partnership. Why?	1	2	3	4	5
3. I believe the partnership helps me get my needs met. Why?	1	2	3	4	5
4. I believe I help my partners get their needs met. Why?	1	2	3	4	5
5. It is easy for me to express my needs to my partners. Why?	1	2	3	4	5
6. I believe my partners trust me. Why?	1	2	3	4	5
7. I believe I behave in a trustworthy manner. Why?	1	2	3	4	5
8. I believe my partners behave in a trustworthy manner. Why?	1	2	3	4	5

Step 2: Develop a Joint Strategic Plan

Once you have determined that trust is moving in the right direction, it is time to begin the task of mutual strategic planning. This requires a high level of trust between partners. During strategic planning sessions, we reveal to our partners our plan of how to achieve our vision. As you share this critical information, you must trust it will be used by partnership members to build a mutually interdependent future.

Strategic planning is the best way to envision what will happen in the next few years. Since you are now in a position to capitalize on the partnership, it is important that you plan what it is you want to do (strategic plan) and how you are going to accomplish it (tactical plan).

When partners strategically plan together, the synergy created is enormous. Your competitors can't replicate your outcome because it exists in the context of your partnership. No matter how hard they try, they cannot recreate that set of dynamics that are uniquely yours.

Before we begin, review the joint Strategic Framework you and your partner created earlier (see pp. 221–23 and the template on p. 180). Is it still viable for the future? If not, what has to change to make the framework a relevant document? Your vision statement, mission statement, or strategic directions may need updating.

Strategic Planning for Partners

There are many excellent resources available to those who want to understand the techniques for developing a strategic plan. The key difference in our case is that when planning within a partnership, you must have your partner present to engage in the activity. This does not mean that you cannot conduct strategic planning without your partner. However, once you have committed to partnership, you must invite your partner into the planning process as it relates to the partnership's activities.

The outline provided below helps partners develop the most value from their partnership. Based on the Holistic Organizational Model discussed in Chapter 8, it explores both the ethereal and material realms of each business and how those two separate entities will support each other as they create the outcome, product, or service they want to deliver.

Recall the elements of the Holistic Organizational Model and the Strategic Framework as follows:

- **Vision statement.** This statement describes where you want to be. It is an altruistic version of how the organization sees itself in the future.

- **Mission statement.** This statement describes in a broad sense how you intend to achieve your vision. It acts as the bridge between the ethereal energies of the organization and the material production.

- **Strategic directions.** Strategic directions define the areas of concentration in which the partnership will be engaged.

The following concepts arise from the Strategic Framework as related to the Holistic Organization Model:

- **Culture:** the quality of the environment in which the partnership resides

- **Goals:** the outcome of the partnership, which is generally planned eighteen to thirty-six months in advance

- **Objectives:** short-term metrics used to monitor progress toward goals

- **Strategies:** individual plans that define how the partnership will achieve its goals

- **Tactics:** specific, targeted activities that help accomplish the strategies

- **Processes:** the work steps within an organization used to accomplish tasks

- **Roles/responsibilities:** the specific tasks and accountabilities the people in the partnership are responsible for

- **Relationships:** how people within the culture work together to accomplish task objectives while building trust and mutual benefits between members

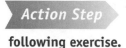 **Action Step** Start by understanding the value proposition that brought the partnership together by completing the following exercise.

INITIAL PROJECT SUMMARY

What were we trying to accomplish?

_____

_____

What was the purpose of the partnership?

_____

_____

Which external customers benefited from the partnership?

_____

_____

What were their needs?

_____

_____

What did we learn about our customers in our initial project?

_____

_____

What did we learn about ourselves in our initial project?

_____

_____

USING THE STRATEGIC ACTION PLANNING MATRIX

Referring to our definitions of elements and concepts above, both partners can now fill out their side of the Strategic Action Planning Matrix below, based on their own experiences and needs from the partnership. After both have completed their portions, the partners should meet and review their responses. What are the commonalities? What are the differences?

Work with your partner to complete the Strategic Action Planning Matrix that follows and share responses when you are finished.

STRATEGIC ACTION PLANNING MATRIX		
Activity	**Partner 1**	**Partner 2**
Vision statement		
Mission statement		
Strategic directions		
Culture		
Goals		
Objectives		
Strategies		
Tactics		
Processes		
Roles/responsibilities		
Relationships		

After reviewing the needs of both partners, you are ready to build a joint strategic plan for the partnership.

Action Step With your partner complete the Joint Strategic Plan Worksheet that follows. This exercise is your first step in developing a strategic plan.

JOINT STRATEGIC PLAN WORKSHEET	
Activity	**Joint Strategic Plan**
Vision statement	
Mission statement	
Strategic directions	
Culture	
Goals	
Objectives	
Strategies	
Tactics	
Processes	
Roles/responsibilities	
Relationships	

VALUES AND ETHICS

Smart partners know it is important to look beyond the immediate relationship to determine long-term compatibility. We do this by investigating organizational values and ethics.

Referring to the sample as needed, with your partners complete the Partnering Values and Ethics List that follows. In this exercise, the partners list their home organization's values and ethics. Then the lists that the partners developed individually are placed side by side and compared. What are the similarities? What are the differences? Are the differences extreme enough to cause major problems in the relationship down the road?

SAMPLE PARTNERSHIP VALUES AND ETHICS LIST

Values/Ethics: Partner 1	Values/Ethics: Partner 2
Integrity	Security
Trust	Safety
Client confidentiality	Trust
Honesty	Client confidentiality
Rigorous analysis	Honesty
Loyalty to client	Friendliness
	Community involvement

PARTNERSHIP VALUES AND ETHICS LIST

Values/Ethics: Partner 1	Values/Ethics: Partner 2

In the sample you will note that there seem to be no large gaps in the two partners' values and ethics. However, there was some discussion around the value of community involvement for Partner 2 and the seeming lack of it for Partner 1.

CULTURAL ENVIRONMENT

The quality of an organization's cultural environment must be considered when planning strategically.

Action Step — The Partnering Cultural Environmental Assessment was created to give insight into the issues that might arise from differences between organizations' cultures. Referring to the sample as needed, complete the assessment that follows to examine the differences between the two organizations.

SAMPLE PARTNERING CULTURAL ENVIRONMENT ASSESSMENT

Cultural Environment	Partner 1	Partner 2
Organizational morale	High	High: leadership Medium: employee
Understanding of mission	High	High
Level of stress	High	Low
Level of acceptable risk-taking	High	Low
Comfort with Self-Disclosure and Feedback	Low	Medium
Conflict resolution style	Win–Win	Competitive
Ability to Trust	Medium	Medium
Past/Future Orientation	Future	Past
Comfort with Change level	High	Very low
Comfort with Interdependency level	Highly independent	Interdependent

PARTNERING CULTURAL ENVIRONMENT ASSESSMENT		
Cultural Environment	**Partner 1**	**Partner 2**

Now let's review the sample in more detail to see how to make use of the information the assessment provides. Based on this information, the partnership decided that before they launched whatever joint marketing initiatives they were planning, they needed to do some work. For example, the Comfort with Change level rating indicated that Partner 1 managers were comfortable with change, but the Partner 2 managers would have more difficulty integrating new products and services into their daily work. The team decided to provide extensive course offerings to help increase familiarity with these products.

ORGANIZATIONAL STRUCTURE

After gaining an understanding of the culture and ethics within the partnership, partners can review the more material areas of the businesses. For your first step, review compatibilities and differences that would help or hinder the partnership from a structural perspective.

Action Step With your partner, refer to the sample below and complete the Partnering Organizational Structure Matrix that follows to describe structural issues pertaining to particular components of the organization. Then share and discuss your responses to this exercise and implications for your partnership.

SAMPLE PARTNERING ORGANIZATIONAL STRUCTURE MATRIX

Organizational Structure	Partner 1	Partner 2
Organizational hierarchy	Bureaucratic	Network based
Reporting relationships	Hierarchical chain of command	Casual-needs based
Communication patterns	Top-down	Horizontal, open
Decision-making methodologies	Autocratic	Consensus
Reward structure	Pay for performance	Team incentive
Marketing initiatives	Industry segments	Regional
Accountability systems	Formal feedback	Weekly updates
Organizational norms	Command and control-no disagreements	Open disagreements-consensus decision making
Legal and regulatory issues	State and federal controls	None
Research and development issues	None	Affiliation with technology institute
Informational technologies	Mainframe-legacy	Network-based PCs

PARTNERING ORGANIZATIONAL STRUCTURE MATRIX

Organizational Structure	Partner 1	Partner 2
Organizational hierarchy		
Reporting relationships		
Communication patterns		
Decision-making methodologies		
Reward structure		
Marketing initiatives		
Accountability systems		
Organizational norms		
Legal and regulatory issues		
Research and development issues		
Informational technologies		

EXTERNAL IMPACTS

The final area of information that needs to be discussed and assessed before the partners can begin a formal strategic planning session involves external impacts on the partnership.

Action Step   **Referring to the sample matrix on the next page, with your partner complete the External Impacts on the Partnership exercise that follows. In this exercise list the external influences that could potentially derail your partnership. When finished, discuss any implications they might have.**

SAMPLE EXTERNAL IMPACTS ON THE PARTNERSHIP

Organizational Structure	Partner 1	Partner 2
Board of directors, owners, stockholders	SEC reviews, quarterly earnings	Privately held
Clients and customers	Consumer products and services	Business to business
Governmental regulatory agencies, accrediting organizations	Public regulatory, environmental protection, safety	None
Suppliers	International	Local
Unions, employee groups, professional associations	Union	Non-union
Political groups	None	Lobby leader in technology
Communities	Poor perception	No visibility
Competing organizations	Many national and international competitors	3 competitors

EXTERNAL IMPACTS ON THE PARTNERSHIP

Organizational Structure	Partner 1	Partner 2
Board of directors, owners, stockholders		
Clients and customers		
Governmental regulatory agencies, accrediting organizations		
Suppliers		
Unions, employee groups, professional associations		
Political groups		
Communities		
Competing organizations		

Sharing of Information and Resources

Once you have built a level of trust, you can begin to confidently share information and resources with each other. Partners can invest in each other's success and achieve more together when they consider two key questions:

1. What potential areas of information sharing exist between partnership members?

2. What potential areas of resource sharing exist between partnership members?

Organizational Ownership of Success

Organizational ownership of success—also known as interdependence—occurs when organizations make the paradigm shift from "me" to "we." We move from independence to interdependence. When an organization has increased its PQ enough to understand that its success is dependent on its partner's success, it takes ownership of the partnership. The partnership is integrated into the culture of the organization. It is now the "way things are done around here."

The more skilled the partnership is in using the Six Partnering Attributes, the higher the quality of relationship between members will be. These attributes are portable: you can use them in many different settings. When employees learn to improve them on the job, they will use those same skills not only between themselves, but also when working with customers and in their personal lives. Employees show higher morale and cultivate better relationships when they communicate more effectively. These elements lead to increased productivity. Since business relies on relationships, customers will continue to support organizations with which they have built a good relationship. The organization wins in many ways.

Step 3: Move to Full Partnership

Our commitment to a full partnership is an ongoing process without which the partnership ends. At this point, we must decide to either expand our partnership or call it quits. Relationships perform, synergies generate mutual benefits, and the partnership thrives. Sustaining growth is the challenge. When partners have reached full partnership, some pretty remarkable things start to happen. You can explore some of the rewards that full partnerships bring to organizations below.

High Trust Enables Creative Risk

Only when we trust each other can we take productive risks. Regardless of the particular service or product, to move beyond what currently exists takes a special talent, and that talent is best achieved through trusting partnerships. Review activities that have occurred because of the high level of trust in the partnerships as well as those that have not occurred due to mistrust.

Open Systems Increase Information and Intelligence

The more information we share, the more we learn. Information growth is exponential; plus we can draw different conclusions from the same information, which makes its importance invaluable. Information sharing exemplifies abundance—there is no limit to how it can be used. Consequently, the more we have and use, the more beneficial it becomes. In reviewing your partnership, ask yourself what open systems and information sharing have occurred within the partnership as well as what systems and information remain off limits, and why.

Partnerships Reap Mutual Benefits

The more people benefit from an activity, the more they are willing to engage in it, and the more success it continues to bring to them. This is a universal truth. It is through full partnership that mutual benefits can be realized, generating wealth for everyone involved. What mutual benefits have been provided to members of your partnership? Has any member benefited more than others, and how? Reviewing these questions enables you to assess the impact of mutual benefits in your partnership.

Partnerships Provide Value Competitors Cannot Duplicate

Don't bet the family fortune on any product or service you may have. Anyone can reproduce a widget. Sooner or later someone will dissect it, figure it out, and make it better. However, competitors can never reproduce the dynamics created through partnerships. This is because each partnership is unique and made up of individuals and interactions. This complex synergy of a productive partnership cannot be duplicated. In this case, two key review quesions should be contemplated. What benefits has this partnership provided to you that your competitors cannot duplicate? And, how can you build on those benefits to beat your competitors in the marketplace?

Win-Win Conflict Resolution Equals Synergy

Organizations that increase their Partnering Intelligence already know how to create win-win conflict resolutions. This ability allows creativity to emerge and generates the "gold" of partnership: synergy. However, to achieve synergy, you cannot apply one or two of the Six Partnering Attributes. All need to be there or the partnership will not move into the creative zone and blast itself away from the competition. Review three key questions: How does the partnership build on the Six Partnering Attributes? Which of the Six Partnering Attributes do you excel in? And, which of your Six Partnering Attributes need improvement?

Continual Improvement

Continual improvement involves reshaping strategies and processes as missions and values change. Accommodating change is an ongoing mandate. All living entities essentially redefine themselves daily by what they do and by the environment they live in. The "full partnership" stage is not the end of the cycle, but ultimately represents the ideal culture in which we work.

We must commit to, and participate in, making our partnerships as full as they can be every day. We will succeed in manifesting our vision by applying these partnering skills not only now, but continually in the future. If we are accountable for ourselves, and if we are intelligent enough to work with others in partnership, we will achieve our brightest and most valued goals.

SUMMARY

Let's review some of the skills you've learned in this chapter.

Stage of Partnership Development—Commit Stage

- **Verifying that trust was built** with all of the partners involved

- **Reviewing your Strategic Framework** for continued relevancy

- **Building a joint strategic plan** for the future

- **Conducting an environmental and cultural analysis**

- **Reviewing values and ethics** to ensure alignment

- **Comparing organizational structure** to expose future problems and implications